GREAT
SEX
MADE
SIMPLE

ABOUT THE AUTHORS

Mark A. Michaels and Patricia Johnson have been teaching Tantra together since 1999. In addition to *Great Sex Made Simple*, they are the authors of two award-winning books: *The Essence of Tantric Sexuality* and *Tantra for Erotic Empowerment*. Their meditation CD set, *Ananda Nidra: Blissful Sleep*, was a 2012 COVR Awards finalist.

Michaels and Johnson have been featured on television, radio, and in numerous publications, including *Redbook*, *Latina*, *Jane*, *Cosmopolitan*, *Woman's World*, the *Sydney Star Observer*, and *Emotion* (Germany). They have also contributed articles to various online and print publications and give sexuality and relationship advice at www.Dick-n-Jane.com.

They are senior students of Tantric pioneer Dr. Jonn Mumford (Swami Anandakapila Saraswati), and have studied Bhakti Yoga with Bhagavan Das and Tantra with Dr. Rudolph Ballentine.

Tantric Tips

to

Deepen Intimacy
& Heighten Pleasure

GREAT
SEX
MADE
SIMPLE

Mark A. Michaels & Patricia Johnson

Llewellyn Publications
Woodbury, Minnesota

FIRST EDITION
Third Printing, 2018

Cover art: Couple: PBNJ Productions/Blend Images/PunchStock
Cover design by Lisa Novak
Interior illustrations on pages 78, 88, 124, 131, 134, 142, 153–154, 162, 165, 168, 171, 193–194 © Mary Ann Zapalac
Interior photographs and art on pages 41, 53, 58, 61, 64, 99–100, 104, 115, 120, 127 by Adrian Buckmaster and provided by the authors

Llewellyn Publications is a registered trademark of Llewellyn Worldwide Ltd.

Library of Congress Cataloging-in-Publication Data
Michaels, Mark A.
  Great Sex Made Simple : Tantric Tips to Deepen Intimacy & Heighten Pleasure / Mark A. Michaels & Patricia Johnson. — First Edition.
     pages   cm
  Includes bibliographical references and index.
  ISBN 978-0-7387-3345-6
  1. Sex. 2. Tantrism. 3. Sex instruction. I. Johnson, Patricia. II. Title.
  HQ23.M4793 2013
  613.9071—dc23
                           2012028483

Llewellyn Worldwide Ltd. does not participate in, endorse, or have any authority or responsibility concerning private business transactions between our authors and the public.
  All mail addressed to the author is forwarded, but the publisher cannot, unless specifically instructed by the author, give out an address or phone number.
  Any Internet references contained in this work are current at publication time, but the publisher cannot guarantee that a specific location will continue to be maintained. Please refer to the publisher's website for links to authors' websites and other sources.
  Cover models used for illustrative purposes only and may not endorse or represent the book's subject.

Llewellyn Publications
A Division of Llewellyn Worldwide Ltd.
2143 Wooddale Drive
Woodbury, MN 55125-2989
www.llewellyn.com

Printed in the United States of America

OTHER BOOKS BY MARK A. MICHAELS
AND PATRICIA JOHNSON

The Essence of Tantric Sexuality

Tantra for Erotic Empowerment:
The Key to Enriching Your Sexual Life

CONTENTS

Part Four: Kissing

Part Five: Awakening the Senses

Part Six: Erotic Trigger Points

Part Seven: Enhancing Oral Sex

Part Eight: Sex Positions: A Tantric Twist

Part Nine: Expanding Orgasmic Response

LIST OF ILLUSTRATIONS

Foreword

While reading this delightful and important book by Mark Michaels and Patricia Johnson, I was overcome by a bittersweet nostalgia. I remembered how thrilling, blissful, and transformative my first Tantric experiences were. I also remembered the challenges of finding teachers with whom I truly resonated. Oh, how I wish Mark and Patricia had been teaching Tantra twenty-five years ago.

I was inspired to study and practice Tantra at the peak of the AIDS crisis, which was having a devastating impact on my friends and colleagues in the New York theatrical community. I did not approach the study of Tantra with the intention of becoming a better lover, or to enhance my relationship with a beloved—even though those things were blissful by-products of my Tantric journey. I began to study Tantra because I was looking for a way for members of my community to be able to have ecstatic sex again, this time more safely. Tantra quickly proved to be an approach that could easily embrace ecstasy, safer sex, and intense love.

But studying Tantra in the 1980s presented challenges. I was told that in order to study Tantra seriously I had to go to India and study with a guru. I had neither the time nor the resources to study in India. I was also extremely suspicious of gurus, especially the type of people who presented themselves as gurus in America. It took years before I understood the difference between the Indian concept of guru as a legitimate spiritual teacher and a Western charlatan.

I was fortunate to meet and study with a wide variety of teachers—none of whom I considered a guru. This deepened my range of experience and knowledge of Tantric practices and sharpened my ability to evaluate teachers and teaching methods. Despite the variety of my studies, I yearned for something more than the form of Neo-Tantra that was being practiced in 1980s America, which was almost exclusively a practice of white, heterosexual, middle-class, middle-aged folks. I yearned—and ultimately had to create for myself—a way of practicing Tantra that included me and everyone else.

You, lucky reader, are far more fortunate than I was. You do not have to piece together your own form of Tantra through experimentation and luck. You do not have to read dozens of books or search blindly for the right workshop to introduce you to the magic of Tantra and Tantric sex. You do not have to quit your job and travel to India. You have Mark Michaels and Patricia Johnson and this authentic, intelligent, and magical book—a book that delivers exactly what it promises: *Great Sex Made Simple*. But it also offers you so much more.

Tantra is a path of love—a radical path of love. I don't mean *radical* as the word is commonly used—meaning extreme or drastic—but rather as the word was originally used, to mean "forming a foundation" or "going to the root or origin." The root or foundation of great sex is not how hot you look in bed or how many positions you can twist yourself into. The secret to great sex—and this *is* truly radical in today's sex-soaked culture—is how present and mindful you can be in each successive erotic moment. For it is only in each present moment—with yourself or with a beloved—that you can reach the heights and depths of the transcendent experiences we all crave.

Mark and Patricia excel at finding irresistible ways to entice us into that present moment. You'll be delighted to find that you don't have to give up your favorite ways of making love—or living life—to practice Tantra. Do you like making love doggy style? Do you love anal sex? Hair pulling? Toe sucking? Mark and Patricia will show you the infinite number of erotic possibilities in all the things you naturally love and desire. You'll soon find that Tantra will become much more than a new skill. It will become a new awareness that will transform not only your sex life, but all of your life.

Mark and Patricia have a deep knowledge of the history and traditional practices of Tantra plus a unique understanding of its essence. Their teaching style is an easy blend of intelligence and simplicity. Their greatest talent is their ability to convey the essence of Tantra in a way that's accessible, appealing, and focused on your pleasure. There is nothing superior or guru-like about them. You'll feel like you're chatting with two old friends over after-dinner drinks. You'll sit in rapt wonder as they unveil the Tantric magic that is possible within even the simplest lovemaking practices, such as stroking and kissing.

Great Sex Made Simple is organized as a sex-tips book, making it easy to find what you're looking for, and allowing you to pick and choose what works best for you. But this is not your typical sex-tips book. Mark and Patricia consistently assume that we all have brains as well as genitals. This is Tantra for smart people. If you thought Tantra was some vague, airy-fairy, woo-woo practice, think again! Would you like to know why Tantra works and where it came from? Do you like your sex—and your spirituality—mixed with a dose of logic and science? I certainly do. It's what I longed for and seldom found in all my early Tantra training. Mark and Patricia never ask us to accept myth or mystery—they teach with a unique and delightful blend of scientific, sexual, and spiritual wisdom.

No discussion of Tantra is complete without its spiritual component. Tantra is, first and foremost, a spiritual practice that includes sex as one of many earthly paths to spiritual awakening. The sexual/spiritual aspect of Tantra is a turn-on for some people, and a source of skepticism for others. Both were true for me when I first began my study of Tantra. My idea of an effective spiritual practice is one in which the spirituality comes to me as an easy and logical result of the practice. I do not have to force it or chase after it. One of the things I have always appreciated about Mark and Patricia's work is their ability to let each of us discover the spiritual and the sexual aspects in our own way and in our own time. As they say, "As is so often the case with great secrets, there really is no great secret. Tantric sex has more to do with your attitude than anything else, so a simple shift in thinking is all it takes. If you can abandon (or at least reduce) goal-orientation and focus on the immediate experience, the rest will take care of itself."

The reason I most wish that Mark and Patricia had been teaching Tantra when I was first starting out is their insistence that Tantra can be enthusiastically enjoyed by anyone of any gender and any sexual or affectional orientation. This idea is less revolutionary than it was when I was first learning Tantra, but it's rarely been endorsed as wholeheartedly as it is in this book. In their embrace of this inclusionary vision, Mark and Patricia are both traditional and transgressive. Historically, transgression *is* traditional in Tantra. As you will read, Tantra has been a highly revolutionary spiritual practice throughout its long history. Mark and Patricia honor that tradition admirably by interpreting that transgressive spirit for a modern world. So, if you have been avoiding Tantra because you didn't think you fit the profile of a typical Tantrika, come on in! We've been waiting for you.

I know from personal experience that trying to explain Tantra or any other embodied spiritual practice in a book can be notoriously difficult. Mark and Patricia have succeeded spectacularly. *Great Sex Made Simple* will not only guide you toward great sex, but the book itself is like great sex: seductive, sweet, satisfying, sublime, and ultimately—sensational.

—Barbara Carrellas

Introduction

Tantra is a notoriously difficult word to define. Our teacher, Dr. Jonn Mumford (Swami Anandakapila Saraswati), favors "tool for expansion."[1] Implicit in his definition is the idea that the physical body can be a vehicle for expanding the consciousness. Others translate it as "web" or "weaving," which suggests weaving the individual consciousness into the fabric of the universe.

When we started doing radio interviews to discuss our first book, *The Essence of Tantric Sexuality*, we were told we should find a way to define the entire tradition in a single sentence—no easy task. We finally arrived at: *Tantra is an ancient Indian tradition that recognizes sexual energy as a source of personal and spiritual empowerment.* Some interviewers got it, but many did not. We would then go on to explain that sexual energy may or may not imply sexual activity (there are celibate Tantric practitioners), but the underlying idea is that sexual energy is the life force, the thing that brought us into the world, and one of the most powerful motivators in our lives. The more we can recognize and embrace this life force, the more fully human and empowered we will be. We have also defined Tantra as: *The magic of transforming your consciousness and thereby transforming your entire being.*

In fact, none of these definitions is fully satisfactory. Tantra is complicated; its history is the subject of scholarly debate, and it was suppressed in its country of origin for centuries. Although Sanskrit is an Indo-European language, and the history of cultural exchange between India and Europe dates back to the era of Alexander the Great, it is almost impossible to project back in time and across cultures to imagine what the early Tantric practitioners felt and believed. Nevertheless, many traditionalists, academics, and skeptics deride the modern, Westernized manifestation of Tantra, either for focusing exclusively on sex or for being "woo-woo": that is, vague, New Agey, and insubstantial.

There may be some truth to these criticisms, but modern, Western Tantra was a great place for us to begin. It is what brought us together in early 1999. The way we started our relationship will probably strike many readers as unconventional, but it has worked out very well for us. We met at Mark's first public lecture on Tantra, exchanged emails for a few weeks, and then went out for lunch. Over that meal, we discussed our mutual interests and decided to start exploring Tantric sexual practice together. There was no drama and no pretense, just the forthright acknowledgment that sex was important to us both and that we wanted to explore it together. We fell in love shortly thereafter, even though neither one of us was looking for a life partner at that time. Our romance was devoid of the emotional volatility that so often characterizes the early stages of a relationship. We started teaching together about six months later and also began exploring more traditional forms of Tantric practice under Dr. Mumford's guidance. We were married in the fall of 2000.

Our work with Dr. Mumford and the initiations he has given us over the years have provided us with a deep understanding and experiential knowledge of inner, nonsexual Tantric practices (which far outnumber the sexual ones), even though most of our work and public teaching have focused on the sexual aspects of the tradition. Our first book, *The Essence of Tantric Sexuality*, is based on lectures Dr. Mumford gave at Llewellyn's Gnosticon Festival in 1976. These lectures were among the first, if not the first, public talks on sexual Tantra given to an American audience by an initiated swami. They inspired many of the popularizers of Tantra who followed and were sometimes borrowed without proper attribution. We were honored that Dr. Mumford allowed us to rework his material and present it to a new generation of practitioners and seekers. Much of the material in that book remains at the core of our public teaching.

Prior to writing *Essence*, we had created an online course entitled "The Fundamentals of Tantric Sexuality." The course was designed to guide people to a direct experience of Tantra through the conscious exploration of their own sexuality. The students who completed the program found it incredibly valuable; some even described it as life-changing. While *Essence* won an award and was very well received critically, some readers who were unfamiliar with basic Tantric concepts expressed a desire for a more basic book. Based on those requests, we took our online course, expanded it threefold, and reconfigured it as workbook; Llewellyn published it as *Tantra for Erotic Empowerment* in 2008. We continue to offer people the option of going through *Erotic Empowerment* with our feedback via email, so the book still functions as an online course, albeit a revised and much-expanded one.

Workbooks and online study are not for everyone, since they demand a significant commitment in terms of time, effort, and focus. We firmly believe that the Tantric approach to sexuality can benefit virtually anyone—of any gender; totally new to Tantra or experienced; single or partnered; gay, straight, or bisexual. We also believe that Tantric concepts can be conveyed in a way that is accessible and easily understood. With this in mind, we decided to write a book that would present these concepts and make them applicable, without requiring people to embrace the entire tradition or demanding that they spend many hours in study and self-exploration. We live in a fast-paced world, and time is precious. We wanted to write a book that was concise and authentic, and that provided specific techniques and concrete, straightforward explanations. Although there are many Tantra books on the market, we recognized a need for one that met these criteria.

The story of our relationship begins with Tantric sex, and this book is, for the most part, about sexual practices, which are what first attracted us to Tantra. Long before we met, we had both intuited that there was a mystical potential in sex, and we wanted to be able to experience that potential at will. Nevertheless, it is important to bear in mind that while Tantra may include sexual activity, it is not merely sacred sex, and to reduce it to just that is to disregard the vast majority of practices that exist within the tradition, practices that are profound and transformational.

We love sex; it is very important to us, but even the most sexually active person spends only a limited amount of time at it. If you devote two hours a day to making love (only a tiny minority of people can claim to do this) and eight hours to sleeping, you are still left with 14 hours of wakeful living to do. Tantric techniques were developed to enrich and inform all aspects of life. This is true even though many Tantric practitioners recognize sex as a sacred activity, arguably even the most sacred activity of all. Thus, we hope and suspect that some of what you read in the following pages will enrich your life in general, perhaps in surprising ways.

Dr. Mumford spent many years studying in India, starting in the mid-1950s and continuing on and off until the 1970s. Before his retirement from public teaching a few years ago, he regularly returned to India to teach at Ananda Ashram, near Pondicherry. In addition, he immersed himself in various Western occult traditions, and received professional training in chiropractic, osteopathy, and psychology. This background has enabled him to teach in a way that is based on a deep knowledge of Eastern and Western mysticism accompanied by a healthy, hard-nosed appreciation for modern science. We aspire to follow his example in all of our work—to provide our readers and students with an understanding of Tantra that is well founded in the tradition and also concrete, substantive, intelligent, intelligible, and practical.

Because of our interest in giving people readily useful tools for enriching their lovemaking and their lives, without imposing excessive demands, we have used a tip-book format and have tried to present the information in short, succinct chapters. This format struck us as being a very practical one. It is also a considerably older and more traditional approach than you might imagine. Many of the classical Tantric texts are written as dialogues between two deities, with one instructing the other in various practices. The instructions are often short, to the point, and considerably less detailed than the tips in this book. Nevertheless, we like to think that the structure of our book evokes the ancient texts.

We have also sought to evoke the Tantric tradition by dividing *Great Sex Made Simple* into nine parts and writing fifty-four brief chapters, one per tip. The number nine is the number of completion in Indian numerology: each stage in the life cycle is said to take nine years, and most mantras are recited in multiples of nine (most often 108). There are fifty-four letters in the Sanskrit alphabet. (Sanskrit is the sacred language of Hinduism.)

The number has significant symbolic meanings in other cultures and religions as well, and of course there are fifty-four cards, including jokers, in the modern deck. There are also fifty-two weeks in the year, and we imagined that people could put one tip into practice each week, with two extras to start the new year with some added pleasure. As with any of the other esoteric ideas we will be exploring, there's no need to believe in numerology to understand that symbolism and metaphor can evoke powerful, unconscious associations and imbue mundane experience with richer and more meaningful textures.

Although this book is structured as a tip book, the first eight of the fifty-four tips do not describe sexual techniques. It would be more accurate to call them capsule summaries of core Tantric concepts, some of which can be applied to any aspect of your life, not just to sex. Many of the individual tips also include discussions of Tantric philosophy; perspectives on contemporary culture, especially cultural attitudes about sex; and may contain multiple suggestions related to a general practical theme. We strongly encourage you to begin by reading the first nine tips in succession. This will give you a conceptual framework and a level of understanding that will make the specific tips more effective. After that, you may skip around if you find that works for you, although we have structured the book to be read sequentially. Whichever approach you choose, there is a wealth of material here.

We have written this book with the total beginner in mind, but we hope (and suspect) that even those who are far more experienced and knowledgeable will discover new and valuable insights and techniques that will inform their existing practice. We certainly did as we were researching, experimenting, and writing. On a related note, because of the format and for the sake of simplicity, we have used endnotes rather than footnotes. If you wish to deepen your understanding, the notes and bibliography include many excellent resources for further reading about Tantra, from both practical and academic perspectives. Regardless of how much you know or how experienced you are, the most important thing is to embrace the practices that work for you—the ones that make your life and relationships richer, more rewarding, and more fulfilling. We think you will find quite a few of them in the pages that follow.

Enjoy!

PART ONE

The Fundamentals: Key Concepts and Attitudes

Tantra can seem arcane, daunting, and alien to the beginner. Books, magazine articles, websites, and workshops often make grandiose promises: sexual marathons, bigger and better orgasms, deeper intimacy, increased longevity, and even enlightenment, all of which can seem very alluring. But too often, these promises go unfulfilled. Readers and workshop participants may find themselves baffled or without practical skills for achieving such lofty goals. We certainly experienced this in our early explorations, so we think it is important to save you time by providing some basic facts, eliminating some misconceptions, and sharing some of the fundamental principles behind Tantric sexual practice. The principles are quite simple, and you can start using them immediately, with very little effort.

Tantra is a spiritual tradition that is over 1,500 years old. It is diverse, has no central authority, and is generally nondogmatic. It is most commonly associated with the religions of the Indian subcontinent and the Himalayas: Hinduism, Jainism, Sikhism, and the Tibetan Buddhist and Bön traditions. Tantric thought may also have influenced some of the more liberal and mystical forms of Islam. In Tantra, the oral tradition and the transmission of knowledge from teacher to student have always been paramount. Texts are useful, but only as adjuncts to oral teachings and what is directly experienced. Because Tantra has a strongly subversive, unorthodox, and even transgressive quality, it was often practiced in secret. Many of the texts themselves are written in what some call "twilight language," with esoteric (hidden) meanings that are not readily apparent to the uninitiated and that are still the subject of debate, many centuries after the texts were composed. There is thus a long history of secrecy associated with Tantric practices, whether or not they involve sexual activity.[2]

This history of secrecy continues to manifest itself in the twenty-first century, although in a different form and mostly for different reasons. If the Tantric practitioners of old kept their activities clandestine because they violated cultural norms, secrecy plays a different and somewhat more vexing role today. This is true both in the West and in India; the word *secret* has been used to sell our work in both parts of the world. The Indian edition of our first book was published under the title *Secrets of Sacred Sex*, and one of our instructional films was entitled *Advanced Tantric Sex Secrets*.[3] Like sex, secrecy sells.

This modern emphasis on secrecy as a marketing tool affects the way Tantra is taught. In some schools, if you just sign up for the next workshop, you'll get the secret teachings, the special initiations, and ascend to the next level. There is some validity to this way of sharing information. Education, whether intellectual or practical, depends on starting with the basics. This enables the student to build a strong foundation before learning more advanced techniques, but that is very different from dangling the promise of secret knowledge or even enlightenment for the purpose of making money. We are not suggesting that teachers deserve no compensation for their time and effort in sharing their knowledge; however, if our book inspires you to learn more about Tantra, we encourage you to trust your own wisdom and be very wary of anyone who tells you that great secrets will be revealed as soon as you part with a few hundred or a few thousand more dollars and sign up for the next workshop.

Given this emphasis on secrecy, people sometimes find themselves groping for that great hidden key that will open the world of Tantra, with its promise of bliss, ecstasy, and sexual marathons. Bliss is likely to elude you if you pursue it too avidly. Don't worry about it, and don't let the desire for lovemaking marathons get in the way of your enjoyment of where you are right now. Not that there's anything wrong with trying to improve your sexual encounters, or any aspect of your life, but if you can abandon (or at least reduce) goal-orientation and focus on the immediate experience, the rest will take care of itself. If you go within, you're likely to arrive at a deeper and more genuine kind of satisfaction.

As is so often the case with great secrets, there really is no great secret. Tantric sex has more to do with your attitude than anything else, so a simple shift in thinking is all it takes. Sex begins in the brain, and becoming familiar with a few important principles can make it easier for this shift to occur. This is also important because it will provide a context for the skills you will learn in later chapters. Understanding these key concepts will not make you an expert on Tantric philosophy (that can take years of study), but it will give you a foundation so that you can make the most of your new knowledge and apply it skillfully.

CHAPTER ONE

Honor Each Other

From the Tantric perspective, each and every one of us is a manifestation of the divine. But the process of living has separated us from this awareness. We've forgotten our own divinity. Before we can truly worship another, we have to learn to worship ourselves.

Embracing this concept can be a challenge. Modern Western society evolved out of a cultural tradition that was monotheistic and dualistic. Even if the Bible says that humans were created in the image of God, we became fallen creatures after the expulsion from the Garden of Eden. Worshipping oneself or another person as an image of the divine is a violation of at least one and arguably as many as three of the Ten Commandments. This is part of our heritage whether or not we had a religious upbringing. We've encountered religious people and atheists who bristle at the use of the word *divine* to refer to a human being. For those religious people, to do so is blasphemous; and for many atheists, divine implies something supernatural, irrational, and otherworldly.

Generally speaking, the distinction between the human and divine realms is less clear in the Hindu tradition than it is in Judaism, Christianity, and Islam. In Tantra, the distinction grows even more obscure. We are at once sacred and profane, at once human and divine, even if we are initially unaware of our own divinity. Awareness is awakened through practice and a form of very deep roleplaying.

Tantric practitioners are guided through a process of identification with a deity, which is chosen by a spiritual teacher based on the aspirant's personal qualities. This process is an imaginative one, involving various meditative techniques including visualization and the chanting of mantras. The literal translation of *mantra* is "mental tool," and the word generally refers to syllables, words, or phrases that can be recited aloud, subvocally, or mentally as a meditative practice. In this context, however, mantras are syllables that relate to the particular deity. Similarly, in Tantric sexual ritual, participants worship each other as manifestations of God and Goddess.

If you've read anything about Tantra or have seen it depicted in movies or on television, you may have heard the words *Shiva* and *Shakti*. Shiva is one of the three main gods in Hinduism, and Shakti is a general term for the Goddess. We will go into more detail about these terms in later chapters. For now, it is important to understand that the participants in Tantric sexual ritual are enacting a microcosmic (small-scale) form of an ongoing macrocosmic (universal) process. They are embodying the God and Goddess, which are believed to exist both within and around them. Although it is probably true that the very early practitioners believed in the literal reality of these deities, they are most easily understood as metaphors—personifications of natural forces—rather than as real beings. Whatever the case, the key point is that in Tantric ritual, practitioners worship each other as divine manifestations.

You don't have to believe in Hindu gods (or any god for that matter) literally or as a metaphor to bring this attitude into all aspects of your life. In Buddhism, there's a concept known as Buddha nature, which refers to our innately enlightened state. Buddha nature is believed to exist within us all, although we may not recognize it. Thus, you can contemplate and honor your own inner Buddha. If you come from a Judeo-Christian background, remind yourself regularly that you are made in God's image. If you are an atheist, you can focus on the beauty of the evolutionary process that made your life possible and revel in your humanity. If you feel attracted to Hindu deities, you can find an image of one that resonates with you and begin to identify yourself with it, by visualizing that image and merging it with yourself. Another simple way to make this concrete is to think of several qualities about yourself that you admire and focus on these qualities for a few minutes a day.

The purpose of this practice is profound. Developing a genuine sense of reverence for yourself makes it easier to revere others and thereby deepen your sense of connection. This is not about self-aggrandizement or feeding your ego. It is about recognizing divine (or sublime) aspects in yourself so that you can see them in others, most especially your partner. If you are single, embracing this quality in yourself, and allowing yourself to be awed by it, will almost certainly make you more appealing.

You don't need a ritual to bring this sense of reverence into your relationship. Nor do you need to reserve the attitude for times when everything is going well. Find a divine spark in your beloved and maintain even just a faint glimmer of that spark in your awareness, whatever the circumstances or your emotional state at any given moment. Your relationship will be richer and stronger for it. This can be a challenge at times, but we have found that it is the key to maintaining a deep and enduring connection.

CHAPTER TWO

Know the Power That Dwells in Your Pelvic Floor

Tantric practitioners have known for centuries that activating the pelvic floor, which encompasses the area between the tailbone and the top of the genitals, is the key to working with sexual energy at its source and that it is very important to bring awareness to and exercise this part of the body. This idea only gained some measure of currency in the West in 1948, when Dr. Arnold Kegel recommended it as a preparation for childbirth and for restoring pelvic strength thereafter. The truth is that Kegel exercises are good for people of all ages and genders, whether they've had children or not.

In Tantra and Yoga there are many different ways to exercise the pubococcygeal, or PC, muscles. These exercises are the first step in a number of advanced energetic practices, since Tantrikas and Yogis recognize the pelvic floor as the very root of human existence, the seat of the life force. The root lock, or *mulabandha*, involves tightening and holding the anal sphincter. Pulsing the anal muscles is called *ashwini mudra* (the gesture of the horse), and pulsing closer to the genitals is known as *vajroli mudra* (the thunderbolt gesture) for people with male genitalia; *sahajoli mudra* (the spontaneous gesture) for people with female parts. (Some traditions do not make the gender distinction and use the terms interchangeably.) This is a very basic overview of techniques that are discussed in considerable detail in several classical texts.

There's no need to memorize the terms or become adept at all the variations, although the more you practice, the more skillful you will become. Focusing on and exercising the muscles of your pelvic floor will connect you with the source of your sexual power, not only because you are toning the muscles but also because you are bringing your attention to this part of the body, something people often neglect. These exercises strengthen erections and make it easier to regulate the ejaculatory response. Similarly, they strengthen the vaginal muscles, improve responsiveness, and help make G-spot or ejaculatory orgasms possible.

You can begin by closing your eyes and bringing your attention to your pelvic floor. Focus as intently as you can. Then inhale, imagining that your inhalation begins deep inside your pelvis. Take five or six deep breaths, maintaining your focus. Next, squeeze your PC muscles; relax them; then bear down (or push out) very gently, so that you feel your labia open or your scrotum descend, working the muscles fully in three steps. The last step is important because G-spot orgasms involve bearing down, which is an unfamiliar movement for some, and because people often overemphasize the contractions, which can produce too much tension.

If you have trouble locating these muscles, you can find them by stopping the flow of urine midstream next time you use the bathroom. Once you've found your PCs and know how to exercise them, try doing three sets of ten pulses three times a day and increase the numbers gradually. This is not only a muscular exercise. By focusing on your pelvic floor, you're bringing attention to your sexuality in a very direct way, and your sexual experiences will be the better for it.

CHAPTER THREE

Collaborate and Take Each Other to New Heights

In conventional sex, many things are left unsaid. People tend to make love with "getting off" as a goal, and they often pleasure their lovers based on an unspoken and frequently unconscious economy of exchange: if you do me for a while, you can expect that I'll do you, and in the end, we'll each get ours (if we're lucky). In other words, people tend to be focused on their own pleasure, and in this context, a partner's pleasure is a secondary consideration.

Tantric sex is very different. Tantric sex is not about getting off (although we're not against that either). Instead, it's about maximizing sexual experiences in order to reach what some would call mystical states. And each person is there to help the other attain that sense of transcendent union.

In Part Two, we'll discuss the way contemporary culture has overemphasized verbal communication, but this is an arena in which talking is invaluable. It is important to break out of unconscious, unspoken patterns of sexual behavior, and the only way to do so is to speak openly and explicitly. If you can't state clearly what you like, either because you don't know or because you're inhibited, there's very little chance that your partner will be able to give it to you, at least not on a regular basis.

If you can freely express your desires and preferences, you can begin to develop a collaborative approach. Of course, you have to know what gives you pleasure and find the way to express it, clearly, kindly, and at the appropriate time (usually not while you're in the act, since sexual arousal is accompanied by emotional vulnerability, and ill-considered remarks are likely to hurt more than they would if uttered in another context). If you can reframe your relationship as a collaboration, in and out of bed, it will be much easier for you to communicate, since sharing your thoughts and feelings will benefit you both. Sharing thoughts and feelings is important, but thinking of relationship as a collaboration is a radical reframing that can be transformational.

In Tantric sexual ritual, the role of each participant is to take the other higher, not with the expectation of getting anything in return, but out of a desire to facilitate the other's erotic expansion and access to altered states of consciousness. Remember that the participants in this ritual worship each other as embodiments of the divine, so an attitude of devotion, reverence, and selflessness is essential. We strive to bring this collaborative attitude not only to our lovemaking, but also to virtually every aspect of our life together. It has enabled us to travel the world teaching, to write books, to share a magnificent sex life, and to have a dynamic and constantly evolving relationship.

Thinking of sex as a collaborative process can open up new possibilities. If we are just seeking (or hoping for) our own personal gratification, we can easily fall into disappointment when a partner fails to fulfill our desires. We've heard people say absolutely brutal things to one another. "You never touch me right" is a common and particularly disturbing example. This statement is at once blaming and disempowering. Nevertheless, we understand why people say such things. They are angry and disappointed because they have accepted a flawed model of relating. If each partner can genuinely embrace being a facilitator, and if both can shift toward a view of sex as a shared adventure, it is unlikely that feelings such as these will emerge.

This is true not only in the realm of sex. We like to apply the model that originated in Tantric sexual ritual to every aspect of our lives. Relationships can be difficult: there will inevitably be some conflict; there will inevitably be periods when things go less well than they do at other times. Trying not to be self-seeking, remembering that your relationship is a collaboration, and maintaining an attitude of reverence and service will empower you, change the way you experience the difficult times, create more harmony, and bring you deeper satisfaction when things are going well.

CHAPTER FOUR

Take Your Time

We live in a fast-moving world, and the pace seems to be ever increasing. The saying "Time is money" may be a cliché, but it reflects a cultural reality: society doesn't value slowing down and savoring anything. There have been some efforts to challenge this norm—the slow food movement is a particularly admirable example—but these efforts at resistance have done little to change society as a whole. Many people yearn for a simpler, more relaxed way of living, but hardly anyone can deny enjoying the benefits of speed in one way or another. The challenge lies in finding a balance and in being able to choose to slow down.

The average American sexual encounter is very brief, usually consisting of a little foreplay and then what is often called friction sex— rapid and mechanical thrusting aimed at producing orgasm, and soon. Some people disparage friction sex, and some educators have borrowed the slow food concept and made an effort to apply it to sex. Two books with the title *Slow Sex* were released in 2011, and some advocates of the approach imply or flatly state that it is a better way to make love.[4] We disagree and believe that suggesting one form of sex is better than another is dogmatic, unhelpful, and potentially shaming, particularly for those who have different tastes or patterns of response. There's nothing wrong with slow sex, nor is there anything wrong with quickies. In fact, we enjoy them frequently, but there's no need to rush your lovemaking every time.

The traditional Tantric sex ritual lasts for hours. We'll explain what we see as the most important reason for extending your lovemaking in our discussion of prolonging arousal. For now, we'll point out that the ritual involves periods of stillness and meditation as part of intercourse. Incorporating periods of stillness into your lovemaking can put you into a meditative state, produce a powerful feeling of connection, and provide you with an opportunity to be together in a new way. You are likely to enjoy subtle textures of experience that are generally unavailable in more intense and fevered encounters.

Sex is a great mystery, and every experience is an opportunity to discover something new. This is true even if you've been with the same person for years. People return to sex again and again, not because they are trying to get it right once and for all so that they can be done with it, but for a myriad of reasons—pleasure, intimacy, and procreation, to name a few. The Tantric approach adds another dimension. It embraces pleasure and the bonding that can take place when we make love and also recognizes that something even more profound is possible. Try taking some time to notice every pleasurable moment along the way. If you rush to get it over with, you're likely to miss a lot.

Most people have orgasm as the goal when they make love. Orgasms are great. We certainly enjoy having them, but sex is about a lot more than just coming. Savor the journey to your climax. Take it slow, especially if you are used to friction sex. You're likely to discover new, subtle sensations and nurture a deeper intimacy in the process.

There's an old saying, "The path is the goal." If you can apply this principle to your sexual life, you're likely to enjoy it a lot more, and if you can focus on what's happening in the moment, instead of on the outcome, you're sure to encounter some new and interesting possibilities. You might even find you've crossed over into new territory—a realm of more satisfying experiences and more gratifying orgasms—whether the sex you're having is fast or slow.

CHAPTER FIVE

Build Excitement and Prolong Arousal

There's an old joke that includes the phrase "Oh God, oh God, I'm coming" as the final build-up to its punchline. This expression is very widely used in fan fiction and erotic literature, to the point of being a cliché, for reasons that should be intuitively obvious but that often go unexamined. Whether it is used in jest or to titillate, the saying has deeper implications, and it evokes a core Tantric principle.

In a very real sense, coming is a gateway to an inner heavenly realm. Recent research suggests that the part of the brain that registers or generates mystical experience is active during arousal and orgasm. Thus, modern science is starting to validate what the ancient Tantrics understood—that orgasm is one of the mystical states most readily available to ordinary people.[5]

They also understood something that is perhaps more important: that orgasm is just the starting point. Tantric sexual practices are aimed at making these mystical states available long before orgasm takes place and also at allowing them to linger after the few seconds of peak experience have passed. This is accomplished by prolonging and building arousal, which is why Sting boasted about making love for seven hours at a time and why popular representations of Tantra place so much emphasis on extended lovemaking sessions, lasting several, if not seven, hours. These representations are not wrong, but they are misleading. We have already suggested that applying Tantric principles to sex involves an effort to abandon goal-orientation, so that you can enjoy and be aware of each moment of a sexual encounter for its own sake. Focusing on goals, whether the goal is orgasm or displaying your sexual stamina, will limit or eliminate your ability to enjoy and be aware. Prolonging arousal is a tool, and that's all.

This is not to say that marathon lovemaking sessions are a bad thing. For most people, they are very pleasurable, and longer periods of arousal do lead to more deeply altered states of consciousness. The truth is: you don't have to go on for all that long. The changes in consciousness that accompany prolonging arousal can be felt quite distinctly after approximately half an hour. They can be felt regardless of what kind of sex you are having and are not limited to intercourse. Although intercourse is not necessary, most people will require some direct genital stimulation to reach or maintain the level of arousal that is needed to produce the altered state.

Thus, it is important not only to prolong the arousal but also to try to build it and maintain as high a level of excitement as you can, even at the risk of losing control. Forty-five minutes of moderate arousal is probably less effective than thirty minutes of being more intensely turned on, especially if you are overly focused on trying to restrain yourself. We don't recommend distracting yourself by thinking about baseball scores, the weather, or anything other than what you are doing.

Alternating between stillness and motion can make it easier to prolong your encounters and can help cool things down slightly if you've gotten a little too excited and are about to go over the edge. If you are already multiorgasmic, you may notice a slight decline in the intensity of your arousal after each orgasm, something that shows up as a wave-like effect on a graph (although some people experience a build-up from one orgasm to the next). These drop-offs are fine, provided they are not too steep and you can get back to a high level quickly.

Experiment with building your arousal for thirty minutes or more. See how high you can go during that period. We suspect you'll feel quite blissful as a result. When you do have an orgasm, it's likely to be a powerful one, and afterwards you may feel more energized than you normally do. Take note of how different the entire experience makes you feel. The difference may be subtle, but it will almost certainly be noticeable.

CHAPTER SIX

Be Present

Being present can be a slippery term. It is widely used in both spiritual and psychological contexts—being present in the moment or being present to what feelings come up for you. One of our teachers, Bhagavan Das, famously advised Ram Dass to "be here now." Ironically, in absolute terms, scientific research shows that this is impossible—by the time we process any experience or sensation, it is actually in the past.[6]

It is sometimes worth trying to do the impossible. This is especially true because we live in an age of distraction. People read while exercising, check email while talking on the telephone, or even worse, text while driving. No one is exempt from the realities of modern life, and thus it is even more important to develop your capacity to be present, even if you are actually being present in a moment that has just passed.

It is probably easier to find examples of being present than to define it. Think of times in your life when you have been totally absorbed in some activity, when you have been completely focused on and aware of what you are doing, with no intrusive thoughts. Think of conversations you've had with someone who seemed to be thoroughly immersed in your exchange and how that person's complete attention affected you. Think of the best sex you've had in your life, when you and your partner were so absorbed by your lovemaking that time seemed to stop and everything else disappeared. Think of those moments of pure feeling, good or bad, when the feeling was all that existed for you. That is what being present is all about. Many

Tantric practices are designed to develop and refine this ability, to make it possible for you to choose to be present when you wish to do so, in a sexual context or in any other aspect of your life.

Tantric practitioners strive to become facile with their awareness, cultivating the ability to be in tune with their inner states while also being attentive to their partners. Many nonsexual Tantric meditations involve exploring the interplay between being outwardly focused and withdrawing one's awareness as fully as one can. Some involve reversing figure and ground by focusing on the spaces between objects (what artists call "negative space") rather than on the objects themselves. Other forms of meditation, such as gazing at a candle flame, are designed to develop one-pointed concentration (that is, complete and undistracted focus). It's valuable to cultivate these skills, since life is an ongoing dance between the internal and the external. Relationships always require finding a balance between connectedness and solitude, and life requires finding a balance between presence and absence.

People often wonder what it takes to become a better lover. They may believe that there are specific techniques that can be learned and that mastering them will guarantee success. Techniques can be useful, but even if we know where the buttons are located and which ones to push, merely pressing them over and over won't make the elevator arrive any faster.

The key to becoming a better lover lies in developing the ability to pay attention. This may sound simple, but arousal can be intense. It is easy to be so absorbed by your own excitement or so consumed by your desire for gratification that you lose awareness of your partner's state.

Paying attention is worth the effort. By remaining attentive and more focused on your partner's pleasure than on your own, you will become a more skillful lover than anyone who has learned a variety of moves by rote.

If you learn to observe the way your partner responds, you can orchestrate your encounters so that you both reach new heights of ecstasy. Without attentiveness, technical skills are likely to fail you, but in the hands and body of a lover who is truly present, techniques can be the tools of a master.

CHAPTER SEVEN

Shed Your Inhibitions

Becoming less inhibited will improve your sex life and make you a better lover. Classical Tantric sex rituals are designed to free the adept from the restrictions that prevail in orthodox Hindu society. These rituals involve eating fish and meat, consuming alcohol, and having unconventional sex, sometimes across caste lines. In ancient times (and even today, in certain circles) to do these things was to violate some of Indian society's strongest taboos.

Members of the *Aghora* (which means "without fear") sect engage in a variety of activities that seem shocking and horrific to the uninitiated, whether Indian or Western, and that violate widely held Indian cultural beliefs about purity and impurity. These include inhabiting cremation grounds; smearing their bodies with ashes from funeral pyres; consuming alcohol, marijuana, and opium; meditating while sitting on corpses; and even eating human flesh from bodies being cremated. While the Aghoris themselves may be fearless, their behavior can seem fearsome to some and disgusting to others. The purpose of engaging in these activities is not only to conquer fear but also to attain a state of non-dual awareness, in which the distinction between sacred and profane ceases to exist. Despite their extreme and socially unacceptable behavior, Aghoris are generally both feared and revered in South Asia.

We are not suggesting that you engage in these specific practices, but we are suggesting that the principle underlying them is a very important one that you can apply to your own life. The Aghori approach is extreme, but the recognition that one should free oneself from cultural restrictions is central in traditional Tantra.

There are a couple of grand rationales for this emphasis on violating taboos. Breaking social rules can lead to an "ah-ha" moment. The shock to the practitioner's system (not the shock to those who observe or read about the behavior) creates a spiritual opening and a new sense of freedom, especially if all the bad things that the practitioner has been led to believe will happen do not. In addition, the idea that facing down demons leads to spiritual powers exists in many cultures around the world.

You don't need to be seeking a spiritual awakening or magical powers to recognize that the less inhibited you are in bed, the better your sexual experiences will be. If you can identify your own taboos, your own emotional edges, and find ways to push up against them, gently, you're likely to become more flexible and open to new delights.

We're not asking you to get out the whips and restraints, at least not initially. If that's what you're into, you won't be pushing your edges, and if it's not what you're into, it's probably not a good choice for a first step. Aghori practitioners go through years of training; pushing yourself too far at first is likely to lead to backlash and may cause you to shut down rather than open up. Begin by examining yourself and trying to identify some personal taboos. Select one that you feel ready to break and see what happens when you do.

For some, this can be as simple as making love with the lights on; for others, it might involve something more complex, like roleplaying or light bondage, or trying some of the suggestions we offer later in this book. Remember that collaboration is another key principle. Exploring your boundaries and breaking shared taboos is a great way to collaborate. It will enable you both to examine and play with your individual and shared edges, to find new pleasures, and to discover what doesn't work for you—not because you've been told it's bad but because you know the truth of your own bodies. To know this is to be empowered. Just make sure that what you do is safe, sane, and consensual, and that it does no harm to others.

CHAPTER EIGHT

Learn to Feel Energy: It's Easier Than You Think

Like the word *Tantra, energy* is a word that gets bandied about (sometimes promiscuously) and that becomes ever more elusive as we attempt to define it. It may have vastly different meanings to different people: nuclear physicists, oil company executives, athletes, or Reiki practitioners. There are people who claim to be able to read it or see it; while some may be on to something, it sometimes seems that these claims are a form of spiritual one-upmanship more than anything else. We hope to give you a very concrete, embodied understanding of the word, because developing a sense of energy is an important aspect of Tantric practice, and thinking about sex in energetic terms is beneficial, whether or not you believe in some of the more mystical ways of defining it.

From the Hindu Tantric perspective, the entire universe is an energetic process, imbued with inert consciousness, figured as the masculine principle or Shiva, which is brought into activity by energy, figured as the feminine principle or Shakti. Note that these polarities are conceived of as masculine and feminine, but they have nothing to do with physical gender. In Buddhist Tantra, the polarities are reversed: wisdom, the analog of consciousness, is the feminine principle, and compassion, the analog of energy, is masculine. These traditions are very closely related, so it is evident that their views of "masculine" and "feminine" are metaphoric and are not rooted in essentialist ideas about gender roles.

It is believed that each of us contains both these masculine and feminine aspects, and the work of the individual practitioner is to unite these polarities—in the heart. Tantric sex can be seen as being a physical enactment of this macrocosmic principle, with one person taking the role of Shiva and the other of Shakti, without regard to the anatomy of either; while this interpretation of Tantric sexual ritual is not strictly supported by the literature, it is congruent with the underlying philosophy and is absolutely appropriate for modern practitioners.

This has all been very abstract, but we thought it important to give you a brief overview of how energy is understood in the Tantric tradition before making it concrete by giving you a simple exercise. This exercise can serve as a building block for interacting energetically. You may never be able to read anyone's "energy body" (aura), but if you can think about all of your encounters, whether or not they are sexual, as having an energetic component, your experiences are likely to be the richer for it.

To begin, fully extend your arms in front of you, or bend your elbows and bring your upper arms to your sides, while keeping your forearms and hands outstretched, whichever is more comfortable. Close your eyes, and open your palms; turn your left palm up and your right palm down. Squeeze your hands tightly and open them again, twenty-four times. Reverse the positions of your palms, right palm up and left palm down, and repeat the process.

Once you have finished, pay close attention to the sensations in your palms. Chances are you feel some tingling or some heat. That's all we mean by energy.

Next, keep your eyes closed and bring your palms close together; try to recognize a point at which you feel something radiating from one or both of your hands. Gradually move your palms apart, and see if you find the place where they no longer feel connected, as if the "energy field" between them had been broken.

Some will likely think, "All that happened was that the nerve endings in my hands got stimulated." Others may say, "I just increased the blood flow." Neither of these statements is wrong, but consider a different way of understanding the sensation: we've brought awareness to something that is going on inside us at all times. If we think about it from this perspective, everything we do has an energetic component—every glance, every touch, and certainly every sexual act. This slight shift in thinking can produce huge changes in the way we interact, and many of the practices in this book will be more effective if you can keep the energetic component in mind.

PART TWO

Self-Pleasuring

Self-pleasuring (masturbation) can be a very useful tool for understanding, embracing, and expanding your own sexuality. We are not aware of any classical Tantric texts that deal with masturbation. The ritual form of Tantric sex involves a partner. As a matter of philosophy, however, the Tantric model doesn't exclude any form of sexual behavior. In addition, the idea that this partner exists within you is a core principle because each one of us is seen as containing both Shakti and Shiva. Thus, you can still approach masturbation with awareness and reverence and treat it as a Tantric practice.

In our first two books, *The Essence of Tantric Sexuality* and *Tantra for Erotic Empowerment* (both published by Llewellyn Worldwide), we delved deeply into cultural attitudes toward masturbation and the history of taboos surrounding the practice. While these taboos may now be weakening, they remain powerful. Even on podcasts, where censorship is not an issue, we have encountered hosts who stumble over the word. When Oprah Winfrey first broached the topic on her television show, she and her guest, Dr. Christiane Northrup, used the phrase "self-cultivation."[7] This word choice may also have had to do with the fact that masturbation sounds very clinical (we often use *self-pleasuring* for that reason), but the reliance on a euphemism reveals how loaded the subject remains.

It is ironic that masturbation causes so much discomfort; there is a good chance that over the course of your lifetime, you will be your own most frequent sex partner. If you want to improve your sex life with others, it is probably easiest to begin by improving it with yourself. Back in the 1970s, Betty Dodson's brave, trailblazing work on female sexuality and orgasm made it possible for large numbers of women to think about masturbation in a more positive way, but many people with male genitals never got that message and are still prone to think of it as a "quick wank," not an exploration.

Not that wanking is a useless activity. It is a great way to relieve tension and induce relaxation. If magic is the art and science of creating changes in conformity with the will, a quick masturbation session for the purpose of going to sleep is one of the simplest and most effective forms of sex magic.

As we see it, learning to incorporate aspects of sexual Tantra into your life does not mean giving anything up, so there is no reason to stop masturbating the way you always have. As you learn new things, you may change; you may grow; but you should never abandon sexual activities you enjoy just because someone tells you they are not "Tantric." We want you to add on, to expand, and to make new discoveries. Masturbating with awareness—making love to yourself, and exploring your body—is a great way to do just that.

This applies whether or not you are in a relationship. Sometimes people in relationships think of masturbation as a form of cheating, as if self-pleasuring were equivalent to having sex with another person. This belief only has a kernel of truth if masturbation is being used as a way to avoid your partner, or if it is so compulsive that your sexual relationship is suffering. In most instances, it does absolutely no harm to the bond, and for many people it actually increases sexual desire.

This is true even if it is done completely privately; even the deepest, most intimate relationships require some separateness and privacy. At the same time, most of us started masturbating in our teens and did it secretly, so masturbating often seems like a "solitary vice," as it used to be called. There is great value in bringing it out of the shadows, at least at times.

In sum, masturbation is still treated with scorn in many quarters and is usually viewed as being, at best, a poor substitute for partnered sex, but you can transform it into a truly spiritual practice, if you approach it with some measure of openness and an attitude of curiosity and reverence for your body and your pleasure.

CHAPTER NINE

Experiment with Your Breath

The Sanskrit word *prana* means "breath," and it also refers to the energy that exists in the air, both inside and outside our bodies. The word *pranayama* is often translated as control or regulation of the breath, and it can refer to breathing techniques, of which there are many in the Tantric and Yogic traditions. At a deeper level, pranayama refers to the regulation of energy, and the purpose of breathing techniques is to direct the movement of energy within the body. To put it in less esoteric terms, you can use your breath to create subtle and not-so-subtle changes in your physical and/or mental state.

In the context of sexual activity, understanding the power of the breath and using it deliberately can be very effective for increasing the range of experiences that are available to you. You can breathe in ways that amp up your arousal, and you can learn how to use your breath to cool down, when you want to do so. Most of us have habitual ways of breathing of which we are unconscious. Becoming aware of these habitual patterns is the first step in learning to use your breath skillfully. Rather than instructing you in specific pranayamas at this point, we will encourage you to observe and experiment.

Think about how you are breathing at this moment, as you read these words. Now, see if you can recall how you breathe during states of heightened arousal. Chances are they are very different. Next, think about how you breathe immediately before and during orgasm. You may not be able to remember. This is perfectly normal; when we're very turned on, our minds are usually focused on the sensations (if they're focused at all), and self-observation can be a challenge.

Even if you were able to remember the way you breathe during arousal and at the point of orgasm, the next step is to observe yourself in these states. The experience may or may not match your memory, and there is a chance you will find that your breathing patterns in partnered sex are not the same as they are when you are pleasuring yourself. Since partnered sex often involves a subtle feedback loop in which each person's breathing influences the other, it is much easier to focus on your own patterns during self-pleasuring. The presence of another also makes it more likely that you will get lost in the experience, making it considerably more difficult for you to witness your own state.

Once you are confident that you have identified your normal breathing patterns during arousal and orgasm, you can begin to experiment with them. See what happens if you breathe heavily and rapidly through the mouth. This can often intensify the experience, as can making sounds.

As you approach the point of no return, try exhaling as slowly as you can. Empty your lungs completely. Then as you go into the orgasmic release, inhale, again making certain that you are taking in the air as gradually as possible.

See what happens when you take in deeper, longer breaths as you approach your climax. Try to focus on engaging your entire body, and imagine that you are spreading the oxygen you are inhaling to every part of it.

Try taking in shallow, rapid sniffs of air just before you reach the point of no return. The infusion of oxygen may intensify the experience.

Next, hold your breath as you approach the brink; exhale as you go over the edge; and see how that affects the way you come. For some people, this increases the tension at just the right moment and leads to a more powerful orgasm.

You may find that some of these techniques work for you and others do not. The Tantric approach is empirical, so use what is effective and discard the rest. It can be very helpful to develop your own experiments; this will provide you with many insights into your own sexuality. There are countless ways to breathe, although most of us have never given the process much thought. Once you have developed awareness and skill at breathing consciously during self-pleasuring, you are likely to get more pleasure from sex.

CHAPTER TEN

Pleasure Yourself in Front of Your Partner

We have already pointed out that most of us began masturbating as teenagers. Adolescence is an awkward time, a stage when people are confused and perhaps overwhelmed by sexuality. Even if your parents were not shaming or sex-negative, the chances are that you began masturbating in secret and received messages from others that masturbation was at best distasteful, perhaps disgusting, or even sinful. There is a pretty good chance that you often did it in the bathroom, a place associated with excretion and washing up, not an intrinsically erotic space. You may well have tended to rush toward a quick orgasm to avoid detection.

This kind of hurried, secretive activity is perfectly normal and understandable, given these deeply ingrained cultural attitudes and the nature of adolescence. Normal is not necessarily desirable, however, and adolescent patterns can leave a behavioral legacy that is less than optimal, both emotionally and sexually. Secretiveness is often accompanied by shame, and being overly focused on quickly achieving orgasm limits the spectrum of your sexual response and the amount of pleasure that is available to you. While masturbating privately, going for those quick orgasms from time to time, and even using shame as an erotic intensifier are all perfectly fine, sharing your masturbatory experiences can be very liberating, provided your partner is on board and supportive.

Human beings are visual creatures and have been creating erotic art since time immemorial. Almost as soon as new technologies are developed—from the printing press, to photography, to the Internet—they are used to disseminate erotic material, much of it visual.[8] Whether we acknowledge it or not, we are fascinated and turned on by visual erotic stimuli. If we are able to see, we almost certainly want to watch.

Similarly, most of us have some exhibitionistic tendencies, some desire to be seen. We may be quiet, shy, and reluctant to admit these proclivities to ourselves, but they are present in most of us. Masturbating in front of your lover is an opportunity to explore this voyeuristic-exhibitionistic dynamic, and it can be a turn-on for both of you. Pleasuring yourself in front of a mirror can also be a very powerful experience, in part because you are playing the roles of both the observer and the observed.

Beyond the erotic charge you are likely to experience as you pleasure yourself before your partner's eyes (or as you watch), this is also an opportunity to learn and explore. Everyone has a unique way of experiencing sexual pleasure; it doesn't always look like what you see in Hollywood movies (if it is depicted at all) or especially in porn. Watching your partner's way of masturbating can be a wonderful opportunity to learn and to become a more effective lover, and by watching yourself in the mirror, you may discover new things about your own sexual response.

The best way to do this is to set aside a block of time, a half-hour or so, and create an erotic ambiance. Make sure you have plenty of lube on hand and allow this to be an extended session in which you make love to yourself. Do whatever it takes to ensure that the experience is safe, supportive, and mutually enriching. If you wish to talk about your fantasies, that's great; however, some people may find this to be too much sharing.

The person who is watching should maintain an attitude of both interest and tenderness. Getting turned on as you watch is fine, too.

After the session is over, take some time to bask in the afterglow. There is a good chance you will want to talk about the experience, but we recommend saving most of the debriefing for the next day, since people are particularly vulnerable after orgasm. For this reason, it is always good to express positive emotions, but keep it simple and upbeat. The in-depth conversations can come later.

It is important to make sure that each of you has the chance both to see and be seen, but schedule your sessions on different days. This is a great way to bring masturbation out of the closet and reduce or eliminate the negative feelings we have been conditioned to associate with self-pleasuring.

CHAPTER ELEVEN

Use a Vibrator:
It's More Than Just a Sex Toy

Vibrators are becoming increasingly popular today, and the *New York Times* recently reported that condom manufacturers are rapidly moving into this market.[9] This is yet another sign that taboos around masturbation may be weakening. Most contemporary purchasers are likely unaware that the vibrator has a long and interesting history. Back in the nineteenth and early twentieth centuries, it was common for doctors to treat "hysteria" (a vaguely defined "female" mental illness that was not formally banished from the medical literature until 1980) in their patients, bringing them to orgasm by stimulating them manually. While this would be considered criminal today, "pelvic massage," as it was called, led to "hysterical paroxysm," a medical euphemism for orgasm.[10] It is interesting to note that a form of this belief persists among some practitioners of "sexual healing" who contend that genital massage, and especially stimulating the G-spot, leads to the release of stored trauma. We think the reason that people feel better after this kind of session is considerably simpler: orgasm is a release of tension, and it is good for you in its own right.

To return to the subject of vibrators, they were originally developed to make it easier for doctors to perform pelvic massage and induce the desired hysterical paroxysm, thereby enabling them to

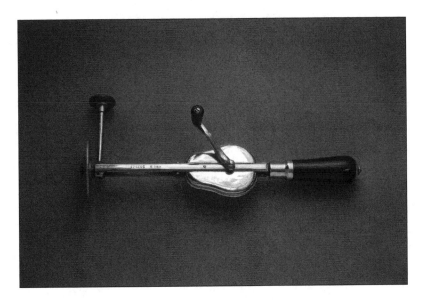

Fig. 1: A hand-cranked vibrator for home use, circa 1900

service more patients and avoid repetitive motion injuries. During that era, medical devices were not nearly as heavily regulated as they are today, so the vibrator soon became available for home use and was sold to the general public through the Sears Roebuck and similar catalogs. It was euphemistically marketed as being good for women's general health. The vibrator remained in this shadowy realm, half sex toy and half muscle-tension reliever, until the late 1960s and early 1970s, when Betty Dodson brought its use into the open. Dodson taught women to masturbate as a way of owning their own pleasure and published *Liberating Masturbation* and *Sex for One* based on the workshops she had been conducting during that era. She deserves great credit for initiating the contemporary trend toward making vibrators readily available, without concealing their true purpose.

You may be wondering what devices that were invented in the modern era have to do with a tradition that is 1,500 or more years old. Chances are the ancient Tantrics never contemplated the invention of the vibrator, although, like erotica, sex toys have been used since time immemorial. From this perspective the vibrator is not so much a modern invention as it is a new manifestation of something ancient.

History aside, remember that Tantra is an empirical and pragmatic tradition. We have been trained to view it as inclusive and open to innovation by each new generation. From this perspective, attitude and approach are what matter, and practitioners are free to use whatever tools are available to them.

The vibrator is one such tool, and using it with awareness and intention can make it a very effective one. The brain doesn't discriminate; it responds when the body is in a heightened state of arousal. Using a vibrator can get you into this heightened state very quickly and efficiently.

There are many different kinds of vibrators available, from small pocket-sized devices to the large and powerful Hitachi Magic Wand. Most people can apply the smaller ones directly to the area being stimulated; the Hitachi may be too intense for some, so you may want to use a pillow or a towel to diffuse the vibrations and moderate the sensation.

For many, direct stimulation of the clitoris is the most effective technique, but you can also try applying a vibrator to the area between your genitals and anus, or just above the pubic bone, which is a way of stimulating the G-spot or prostate externally. Given the history, there is a tendency to think of the vibrator as a tool for women only, but people with male genitals can use them too. You can hold the penis in one hand and apply a Hitachi Magic Wand to your fist. This is likely to be intensely arousing. You can apply one of the smaller versions to the frenulum (the very sensitive area at the head of the penis, beneath the opening of the urethra). If you're already highly aroused, this is likely to send you over the edge. You can also try placing the vibrator below your scrotum while using your hand to masturbate. This will send waves into the prostate and is likely to produce a very powerful response.

There are countless ways to use a vibrator, and it is up to you to discover what feels best. This simple mechanical device can help you explore your erotic response, become more orgasmic, and intensify your partnered experiences. By using one consciously, you will be converting a toy into both a toy and a Tantric tool.

CHAPTER TWELVE

Fantasize Freely

Fantasies, like masturbation, are controversial. In the 1970s sexual exploration was a vibrant part of American culture, and during that time Nancy Friday raised public awareness about the role of fantasy.[11] Friday's books made it socially acceptable to acknowledge having sexual fantasies. Although cultural attitudes regarding sexual orientation and same-sex marriage have evolved rapidly in recent years, generally speaking we are living in a less adventurous, more conservative time, and attitudes toward fantasizing are not as positive as they once were.

In our years of teaching, we have met a significant number of people who feel that fantasizing about a person other than a beloved is tantamount to cheating. We have encountered others who feel ashamed of their fantasy lives. These attitudes seem to reflect a cultural trend that includes the movement to define compulsive sexual behaviors of various sorts as "sex addiction."

Many sex-addiction counselors consider fantasizing as a "boundary" or warning sign that a so-called sex addict is on the brink of relapse.[12] The founder of the sex-addiction movement, Patrick Carnes, identifies fantasy as the first of his ten "types" of sexual addiction and also considers fantasy a primary coping strategy for the sexually addicted. According to Carnes, "Lapsing into voyeurism in fantasy or visiting an old lover may not cause an immediate relapse, but it will certainly grease the slide to get there."[13] Many conservative Christians view fantasy as sinful in itself and corrosive to the marriage bond.[14]

For those who believe in "manifesting" (using the mind to make your desires real), the line between fantasy and reality is often blurry, and fantasizing about something may be seen as inviting that something into your life. These are all beliefs that find little or no support in the scientific literature on fantasy. In fact, one recent British study of sex offenders found evidence that contact pedophiles, those who actively engage in sex with children (as opposed to Internet offenders), often suffer from "fantasy deficit."[15]

Another study, of 19,000 people in Great Britain, found that the vast majority of adults fantasize frequently (96 percent of males and 90 percent of females self-reported as doing so). Most fantasies were about someone other than a current long-term partner; fantasies often involved sadism (inflicting pain on others), masochism (experiencing physical pain, submission, or humiliation), and even illegal violent acts.[16] In our view, there is no harm in having any fantasy, unless it leaves you with bad feelings about yourself or is accompanied by a strong desire or compulsion to act in harmful ways. For normal, mentally healthy people, the purpose of fantasy is to build sexual arousal—that intrinsically mystical, altered state of consciousness. Beyond that, fantasy is an imaginative act, and the richer and more complex our imaginative lives, the fuller and more flexible we will be as human beings.

While the author of the second British study suggested that basic fantasy structures stay the same over the course of a lifetime, it is safe to assume that the overwhelming majority of his respondents had no familiarity with the experimental Tantric approach, with its emphasis on consciousness and awareness. Most people have tried-and-true fantasies that have worked for them for years, and the most common reason for attempting to change a pattern is quite likely guilt over the fantasy itself. We propose an entirely different way of working—the intentional use of fantasy to expand the spectrum of erotic experience (including purely mental experience) that is available to you.

This brings an element of choice and therefore greater freedom into your fantasy life. If you stick with your tried and true, which is tried and true because it works for you, know that you are actively making this choice. When you try out something new, whether it is a kinky scenario, group sex, an encounter that goes against your general orientation, or imagining your body as possessing both male and female genitalia with which you can make love to yourself, think the fantasy through before using it in masturbation. Then do your best to observe how the experience feels for you. Make this a regular practice, and you are likely to become more flexible in your capacity for erotic response. If the preceding suggestions seem a little daunting, it may be easier to begin by adding a new element to one of your favorite scenarios; you can bring the variation in just before orgasm.

We have a couple of additional thoughts regarding fantasy in long-term relationships. Sharing fantasies can be a huge turn-on, but it can be delicate and even threatening for some. If you want to share your fantasies, be sure to do so kindly and in unthreatening terms. Also be sure that your lover is both open to hearing what you have to say and prepared to be kind to you in return.

In the realm of partnered sexual activity, fantasy is a bit more complex, since the Tantric approach to lovemaking involves presence and a collaborative attitude. If relying on fantasy in this context is a way of retreating and interferes with your ability to engage, it is probably not helpful. If you use fantasy to increase your arousal or focus your mind on being sexual, it can be a very effective way to improve your lovemaking experience. This is also true of mutual fantasies, which can be a delightful way to take each other higher.

These few caveats aside, there are no limitations in the realm of fantasy. Virtually anything is possible. Your mind is the place where true expansion can happen, so allow yourself to fantasize and do so skillfully.

CHAPTER THIRTEEN

Change Your Position
to Change Your Experience

Just as many of us have a tried-and-true pattern of fantasizing, people tend to have one or two preferred positions for self-pleasuring. Given the virtually infinite variety of sexual options that are available in the context of masturbation, it is ironic that most of us end up choosing such a narrow range. While operating within that narrow range may bring us much pleasure, we have not approached the full spectrum of possibilities, and there is always the potential to learn something new, even within a realm that we think of as familiar.

Again, this is not a matter of abandoning what works for you; it is about exploration and self-discovery. Some new positions may not bring you much pleasure, but others may give you a very different kind of experience, and possibly even a more enjoyable one. As always, if something does not work for you, especially after several tries, simply drop it and move on.

Sex educators and therapists have long advocated changing positions during masturbation as a way of improving sexual response and sometimes as a way of addressing dysfunction. Betty Dodson also advises women to move while masturbating. (If this is your normal behavior, you might want to try to move as little as possible, just to see what happens.) We certainly support this approach if people are having problems. Moreover, even if you are functional and happy with your sex life, varying positions can be very helpful in terms of gaining a deeper understanding of your erotic response and expanding your capacity for sexual pleasure. To approach this as a Tantric exercise, make the conscious decision to do something different and observe what happens.

If you are accustomed to masturbating on your knees, see what it feels like to do so while lying on your back. If you lie on your back, then try it on your stomach or vice versa. Extend one leg and bend the other. Stand in front of a mirror. Try putting one foot on a stool. There are numerous possibilities, but this is only the most obvious level of variation. Changing your body posture alters your consciousness. This is well known in Yoga and some other traditions, so observe carefully and see how the changes in position affect you.

Some Western Tantric workshops focus on giving people big experiences, emphasizing better, more explosive orgasms and intense emotional and energetic openings. While this has its place and is valuable for some, Tantric practice is also about refining awareness, becoming facile with it, and developing the ability to notice subtle changes. Thus, changing positions is only the first step.

We also encourage you to explore changing the pace of your self-stimulation. If you tend to be a fast and furious masturbator, someone who rushes toward that orgasmic release, slow down, and see how long you can make the session last. See what it is like to use your nondominant hand. If you are used to using a lot of lube or saliva, see how dryer friction feels. Experiment with different implements: fleshlights (sex toys that simulate the vulva and are designed to be penetrated) or dildos (sex toys designed to penetrate); try stimulating another erogenous zone simultaneously (see Part Six).

Stretching your body regularly will make your muscles more flexible. Similarly, breaking old patterns and varying your way of masturbating will make you more erotically flexible.

PART THREE

Beyond Words:
Silent Ways to Create
Intimacy and Reverence

Mainstream and New Age relationship experts often focus on developing communication skills as the key to having harmonious relationships, but in reality, most couples talk either too much, not at all, or only about the mundane details of their lives. Communication is valuable. Sharing mundane details, as well as your deepest thoughts and feelings (although not necessarily all of them), is very important for building and maintaining intimacy. Generally speaking, however, verbalizing is overrated, especially unfiltered venting of your feelings about your partner, something that people often mistake for communication. This kind of self-expression is frequently nothing more than self-indulgence. It usually produces more conflict, not less, and it can interfere with a deeper, unspoken form of bonding.

Try to remember the experience of falling in love (or if you are currently in that heightened state, think about how you and your new beloved interact when you're together). Chances are you could spend hours just gazing at each other wordlessly. That's not to say you didn't talk or that talking wasn't an important part of the process, but falling in love involves a lot more than conversation. Talking enables people to get to know each other intellectually, to hear each other's stories, and to make some judgments about whether they are compatible. These are only the most basic and arguably the most superficial aspects of falling in love. Much of the really important communication that goes on in these early stages of a relationship is nonverbal. It involves body language, the gaze, touch, and a whole array of other forms of expression. We often miss or neglect these elements, or call them chemistry, because so much of falling in love takes place on an unconscious level.

Once we recognize the importance of nonverbal communication, we can take steps to re-create the process of falling in love on a daily basis. This will keep the sparks flying in long-term relationships; build harmony, intimacy, and connection; and make it easier to deal with conflict when it does arise. If you are in a new relationship, using this knowledge will help you build a stronger foundation for the long run (it certainly did for us). If you are not currently in a relationship, bear these concepts in mind the next time you meet someone and feel a sense of possibility. The practices are simple and only take a few minutes a day.

To reiterate, communication is important, but talking is overrated. You can find countless books that are replete with instructions on how to communicate with your beloved. (An Amazon.com book search for the words *couples* and *communication* produced 416 hits.) Many of them are focused on how to get what you want from your partner. You can go to any retreat center in the country and find workshops devoted to communication skills, active listening, and other ways to build intimacy through verbal expression. Some of this information is probably helpful for some people, but we are convinced that the best way to connect is to shut up and do it.

We're not trying to be flippant when we make this assertion. Talking about your problems is not the best way to create or nurture a feeling of connection. More often than not, it leads to polarization and takes you away from your love for each other, since it engages the left hemisphere of your brain, the rational side. Falling in love isn't rational. Connectedness comes first, and creating a feeling of unity is more important than complaining about your partner's failing to meet your needs, or even asking for what you want.

The time to talk about issues is when you're feeling connected, not when you're feeling as if you're on opposing teams. And if you are feeling polarized, resist the urge to express yourselves, and take some time to connect nonverbally. After you've done so, you're likely to find that verbal communication is easier and that you are able to address the issue as collaborators, not adversaries. We've used and taught these techniques for years, and they really work.

CHAPTER FOURTEEN

Gaze into Each Other's Eyes

Eye-gazing is rooted in the traditional Tantric practice of *trataka*, which means "to gaze without blinking," but you can blink during this exercise. In its classical form, trataka often involves focusing on and internalizing the image of a deity. It can be very helpful to bear this in mind when you begin to gaze, because it is an opportunity to see the divine in your beloved. After a moment, let the thought go, and allow pure experience to take over. You will probably go into a meditative state quite rapidly.

This is a deceptively simple and powerful practice. We started doing it on our very first date, and spent a few minutes at it whenever we were together. When we began sharing a home, we did it on a daily basis as a formal exercise. Now, it is second nature to us, and we do it both intentionally and out of habit. We also make an effort to use it when-ever there is a feeling of disharmony between us. Taking a time-out and gazing at each other silently brings us back into balance and defuses conflict. We are able to do this because we built a strong foundation by practicing regularly when things were going smoothly. This gives us the ability to recognize when we're out of synch and to make the choice to pause and connect, rather than allow the disruption to get worse.

Stand facing each other, with your arms at your sides, and gaze softly into each other's eyes. Focus on your partner's left eye with your right, and allow your left eye to relax and receive. Don't worry about your thoughts. In all probability, your mind will start to go quiet after a couple of minutes.

Fig. 2: Eye-gazing is an energetic exchange that involves looking deeply into your partner's eyes. It brings you into alignment by harmonizing your emotional states.

We are aware that people teach this technique in a variety of ways. For example, some encourage either observing your emotions or talking about them while you gaze. We feel it is more effective to keep your full attention on your partner's left eye, as this practice has its origins in a technique that is intended to create one-pointed concentration, the ability to focus intently on one thing without becoming distracted. More importantly, just thinking about, let alone expressing, your emotions in this context takes you out of the moment and will interfere with the harmonizing effect of the practice.

We have also met people who have been taught to gaze left eye to left eye, because the right eye is said to be "aggressive." We have tried this method and do not believe it is nearly as effective for a few reasons. First, it requires you to look at each other with a kind of sidelong glance, which feels awkward to us. Second, in traditional Tantra, the right side is the active, sending side and the left the receptive one, so it makes more sense for us to keep our attention on the sending side while letting the left side passively receive. There's an additional basis for our feeling; it has nothing to do with the Tantric tradition or beliefs about energetic circuits. Research suggests that the left side of the face reveals more about our emotional states than the right.[17]

Focusing the right eye on your partner's left, and hence on the left side of the face, is a much easier and more direct way to see your partner's emotional state because you are looking intently at the part of the face that reveals it. You can't register as much if you're looking left eye to left eye. We also suspect that by keeping your mind on your right eye as you look into your partner's left, you are keeping your brain's left hemisphere occupied with a single task, thereby quieting the mind. Remember that the purpose of doing this is not to read emotions consciously but to create harmony and to renew and deepen your connection.

This practice will bring you into synch. After a couple of minutes, you will have harmonized your moods and metabolisms. Beyond that, you are re-creating the process of falling in love, on multiple levels. Although we think the word *healing* is overused, we suspect that eye-gazing can do a great deal to repair emotional wounds of many kinds, since it replicates perhaps the most primal form of bonding that takes place during infancy—the gaze between baby and primary caregiver.

We also recommend that you gaze into your own eyes in the mirror. Solo gazing is a very valuable thing to do even if you are in a relationship. We've had students who found this form of the practice to be profound and even life-changing; one of them approached us at a conference several years after we'd taught it to him. He told us that gazing into his own eyes in the mirror and honoring himself on a daily basis had transformed him.

Many couples find it challenging to gaze together at first, especially if they've lost the habit of looking at each other. It is not uncommon to laugh or feel some initial unease. These are perfectly natural responses, but if you stay with it, the discomfort will pass, and you should start experiencing the benefits.

CHAPTER FIFTEEN

Keep in Touch

We like to say that lovers are like planets in orbit around each other and that relationships require sufficient gravitational pull if they are going to endure. This gravitational pull has both emotional and physical components. If there's too much distance between the bodies, they'll continue to move away from each other. Your body and your emotions do not exist independently of one another, but for the purposes of this section we're talking strictly about the body and using the body to affect the mind. Remembering and consciously choosing to maintain physical contact can be a very effective way to stay within each other's orbit.

Our teacher, Dr. Jonn Mumford, emphasizes that Tantra is a tactile path, and in Tantric anatomy, the sense of touch is associated with the heart.[18] This is yet another example of just how deeply the Tantrikas and Yogis of old understood the human psyche. We need to be touched almost as intensely as we need food and water. Infants will fail to thrive if they don't get sufficient physical contact, and there is increasing awareness that elderly people, in particular, are starved for touch. This need for touch is just one of the reasons that receiving a massage is so beneficial, and it may be the most important one of all.

Just as people who are first falling in love can spend a long time gazing at one another, they can also seem to be in constant physical contact, and just as long-term couples often stop looking at each other, they often stop touching too. This is true even if the relationship is relatively sound in other ways. This lack of regular physical contact may exist between people who are still sexual together, but the absence of affection is often a sign that all is not well.

People drift apart for many reasons, but we suspect that failure to keep in touch is among the most common ones. There may be no deep emotional issues, just a lack of contact and a gradually widening gap that goes unnoticed until it becomes a chasm. Deciding to stay physically connected will keep the attraction alive. If things are currently good between you, actively choosing to touch each other more frequently is likely to make things even better, strengthen your connection, and nurture a bond that is more likely to endure.

You can choose to maintain or renew a physical connection with your beloved. You should do this on a regular basis, whenever possible. Hug and kiss when you greet each other. Hold hands when walking together. Lie in each other's arms while watching a movie.

Attitudes toward public displays of affection, even mild ones, vary a great deal depending on cultural and familial background. If you come from a background in which touching in public, or in front of children, was discouraged, we still recommend that you make an effort to have regular, affectionate contact. This may involve pushing your boundaries a little bit (remember that this is an important aspect of Tantric practice), or you may choose to reserve this kind of contact for times when you are alone. Either way, we encourage you to find ways to connect physically as frequently as is possible. Regardless of your background or belief system, keeping in touch is a key to keeping any relationship alive and vibrant.

CHAPTER SIXTEEN

Breathe Together

We have already introduced you to some basic Tantric concepts related to the breath and to our view that breathing consciously during self-pleasuring and intercourse is one of the most effective ways to create an expanded experience of sex and orgasm. We will return to this subject and examine it in greater detail more than once in later chapters. If breathing is one of the most effective ways to regulate and direct energy during sexual activity, it is useful in many other contexts as well, including before and after sex. In addition, breathing together intentionally is another very effective way to connect and harmonize.

In the late 1990s, country music star Faith Hill had a huge hit with the song "Breathe." Whether or not this song appeals to you personally, the popularity of Hill's recording reveals not only how intimate breathing together can be, but also the yearning that many people have for the kind of connection this practice inspires. It is another way you can consciously and deliberately act to strengthen your bond, without saying a word.

It can be exquisite to lie quietly in the afterglow of making love and breathe together. You can allow the rise and fall of your lover's abdomen to set the rhythm. This is deeply relaxing and can be far more intimate than most conversation.

You can also use breathing together as a form of fore-foreplay. If you want to be intimate but are feeling a little stressed or out of sorts,

Fig. 3: Seated posture that facilitates harmonizing the breath

taking time to synchronize your breathing can help ease you both into the mood.

There are many different ways to do this. You can do it lying down, as we've already described; you can breathe together in a standing or seated embrace, either face to face or with one of you behind the other; or you can do it standing a couple of feet apart, facing each other. This is often the easiest approach for beginners, because you can use both visual and auditory cues to determine when you are in synch. Allowing yourself to sigh on the exhalation is a clear signal that you are exhaling. It has a very grounding effect and will bring your focus back to your body.

You can also use breathing together while standing face to face in the early stages of the eye-gazing practice, especially if you are feeling strong emotions. Inhale deeply and audibly, through either the nose or the mouth, and then exhale through the mouth with a sigh. This will make it easier for you to match up. It will also help clear your mind and dissipate (or at least take your focus away from) whatever emotions you may be feeling, making it less challenging to eye-gaze, and facilitating your transition into a meditative state.

Initially, making sounds may feel awkward, and that's understandable. Some of the popular portrayals of contemporary Tantra have mocked this very sort of breathing. People are often made uncomfortable by expressive vocalizations, especially when there are no words involved, both in a sexual context and in general. We will have more to say about making noise during sex later, but even in the context of simple exercises like these, inhibition can be a factor.

It may help to think that making sounds is just another way of moving energy. Sighing leads to the release of tension in your body and will make it easier to match up your breathing. The feelings of awkwardness should disappear with a little practice, but if they persist, just try to follow your partner's patterns by relying on visual cues.

Whatever approach you take, synchronizing your breathing is a way to harmonize and to create a calming, peaceful intimacy. This can help defuse conflict, set the mood for a sexual encounter, and be the perfect coda after you make love.

CHAPTER SEVENTEEN

Connect: Hands to Heart

We are not entirely sure where this practice originated. It is a basic human gesture, but it was popularized by Bhagwan Shree Rajneesh (now known as Osho) and his disciples. Osho was not traditionally trained or initiated; he devised his own system that was based on a mixture of his wide reading in spiritual literature, including Tantra and Western psychology. There are many good reasons to be critical of Osho and the movement that he founded, but that discussion is beyond the scope of this book, and there can be no denying that he has had an enormous influence on the way Tantra is taught and practiced in the modern world.

Regardless of what anyone thinks about Osho, it is safe to say this technique is now a staple in most Tantra workshops, in one form or another, and with good reason. It is a very simple way to connect. We have added an additional element to the standard method—one that we think makes it even more effective.

Combining physical touch with looking deeply into your beloved's eyes can create and sustain an even deeper sense of connection, so this practice is best used in conjunction with eye-gazing. Begin by placing your right hands on the center of each other's chests, near the heart. Next, cover your partner's right hand with your left and vice versa. Take several deliberate, audible breaths, sighing on the exhalation. Spend two to three minutes gazing into each other's eyes while performing this heart salutation.

Fig. 4: Heart salutation

As with eye-gazing, don't worry about your thoughts. In time, your mind will go quiet, especially if you deliberately synchronize your breathing. This is likely to happen naturally, but focusing on your breath will help you stay present and add another harmonizing element.

To make the practice even more effective, you can do the hand exercise we described in chapter 8, "Learn to Feel Energy: It's Easier Than You Think." Next bring your hands to each other's hearts. If you can feel the energy flowing in your hands, you can then imagine that you are transmitting that energy to your partner's heart, and vice versa. You have already created an energetic circuit by eye-gazing. You are now creating another one that runs through your arms and into your hearts, so you will be doubly connected. You may even have a faint sensation that your partner's chest is absorbing your hand, and you are merging. Do not force this or try to pursue any specific result. Just allow things to happen.

Like many of the practices we're sharing, the heart salutation may seem a little awkward and formulaic at first, but it is another way to re-create the physical circumstances that led you to fall in love. Think about the times you snuggled together with your hand resting on your lover's chest. This is another way evoke those early moments of intimacy and rekindle your passion for each other.

You may find that this feels so good that you want to do it for more than two or three minutes. We sometimes get so lost that our sense of time warps, and we fall into such a deep state that we don't know whose hands are whose. In conjunction with breathing and eye-gazing, this exercise can help to ground you both and equalize your emotional states. Because this approach engages several senses—touch, hearing, and sight—it is an effective way to short-circuit conflict without saying a word.

CHAPTER EIGHTEEN

Bow to Each Other

If you've studied Yoga or a martial art, you are probably familiar and comfortable with bowing. In those contexts, we are likely to bow not only to the teachers who outrank us but also to our peers. If you have not had this kind of experience or did not grow up in a culture in which it is a normal form of greeting, the act of bowing may seem alien and artificial. It may even seem more alien and artificial than eye-gazing, at least at first.

Bowing, particularly bowing to a peer, is not part of our cultural heritage, and we tend to think of the act as being one of self-abasement, as bowing down. This belief probably has its origins in the Middle Ages, if not earlier, when bowing to one's social superiors was a gesture of deference to their rank. The fact that President Obama was excoriated by some of his critics for bowing to his Japanese and Chinese counterparts, as if he were somehow diminishing his office, illustrates the persistence of this attitude toward bowing in American culture.[19]

The negative view of bowing is unfortunate because this simple gesture is profound, and doing it regularly can be transformational. This is true whether it is a gesture of respect and appreciation for a teacher or a similar gesture directed at a peer. We no longer live in the medieval world, where birth and rank were all that mattered, so bowing is not something we need to associate with submission (unless we choose to do so).

Fig. 5: Bowing is a very effective way to nurture an attitude of reverence

One of our teachers, Bhagavan Das, has described bowing as "ducking" to get your ego out of the way.[20] Bowing to each other simultaneously is an act of parity, not submission or subservience. In the context of an intimate relationship, it is a gesture of reverence, appreciation, and respect: a nonverbal way of expressing your feelings for your beloved, and bringing your own attention to those warm feelings. It is a very simple, physical way to remind each other that your interactions are significant and perhaps even sacred (if you're comfortable applying that term).

Chances are you didn't just spontaneously bow to each other when you were first dating. Unlike some of the other nonverbal techniques we've described, it almost certainly wasn't part of your routine when you were falling in love, but if you can embrace bowing and incorporate it into your interactions, it will help you stay in touch with your positive feelings for each other. Try bowing after doing the joint exercises in this book and especially after making love. Just press your palms together at your heart, and lower your heads. You can gaze into each other's eyes while doing so if you wish.

As we see it, sex is intrinsically sacred. There is no need for you to believe this, but most of us understand that sex is, at a minimum, something special, important, and worthy of respect. It is very easy to take sex for granted, and it is very easy to take our beloveds for granted, especially in long-term relationships. You can also bow to yourself either physically or mentally, as a gesture of respect and honor. Whether done alone or as a gesture toward your beloved, bowing will keep your mind on the value of your lovemaking, your union, and the importance of everything that you share.

CHAPTER NINETEEN

Pay Attention

To a significant extent, all of the techniques we have described in Part Three involve paying attention. Choosing consciously to make use of them requires a willingness to focus on your partner and your relationship, and employing them as techniques for short-circuiting conflict requires you to be acutely aware of your emotional state and the state of your relationship. At the same time, doing these practices, especially eye-gazing, serves to refine and enhance your ability to focus. If you can incorporate them into your daily routine, or even make them something you do several times a week, you will be creating a feedback loop and will likely become more engaged and attentive. Developing the capacity to pay attention is closely related to being present (see Part One, chapter 6).

Our teacher's teacher defined love as "profound interest." He went on to say that the opposite of love is not hate but indifference. Cultivating and displaying interest is essential if you want to stay connected. Paying attention means more than just listening and responding to verbal cues. It means developing the ability to read your partner's moods and maintaining an inner attitude of genuine curiosity about your beloved.

On one level, paying attention does require listening, but it goes far deeper. It involves attending to subtle and unspoken cues and truly caring about what they mean, not because there's anything in it for you but because the person you have chosen to be with is dynamic and ever changing. Focusing on your partner with profound interest will allow you to witness and participate in this wondrous process of personal evolution. It will also enable you to respond with sensitivity to your beloved's desires, rather than being preoccupied with your own.

When one of us says, "I love you," the other will often respond with, "Why?" Our stock answer is, "I don't know. It's a sweet mystery." It's a lighthearted response, but it's no joke. The opportunity to relate intimately with another is awe-inspiring. The experience is a sweet mystery that deserves our full attention.

The truth is that we can never fully know another person, even if we spend years together. The self is not something that is fixed and static. Some aspects of a personality remain fairly constant; others change over time. We are not the same people we were when we met in 1999, even though we know each other very well. There is always room to be pleasantly surprised by some new or previously unrecognized aspect of your beloved's personality.

It is certainly true that sometimes these discoveries are unpleasant, and people in relationships may find that they have evolved in different directions and no longer wish to stay together. That said, we suspect that many instances of people growing apart are due in large measure to a failure to pay attention. If we take our partners for granted or decide that their behavior is entirely predictable, we are likely to miss out on many opportunities to be pleasantly surprised and to feel connected. Conversely, if you can actively cultivate profound interest in each other, you will be communicating your love, and you may discover that you both feel more passionate as a result.

When people are falling in love, they are usually very attentive. They will hang onto a new beloved's every utterance and go to great lengths to learn the likes and dislikes and anticipate the desires of this mysterious other. In the early stages of a relationship, people buy each other flowers and gifts—making sure to show interest and sensitivity, and demonstrating their desire and ability to pay attention. Such attentiveness often wanes as courtship ends and couples grow familiar and comfortable with each other.

You have the power to re-create some of that early enthusiasm on a daily basis. Pick one thing you know your beloved likes, and do it for him or her. It doesn't have to be a big surprise, nor does it have to involve buying extravagant gifts. It can be a small gesture—making coffee in the morning, picking up the dry cleaning after work, drawing a bubble bath before bed, or perhaps even better spending half an hour a day in conversation about something that matters to your beloved. Try this for a week, and see what happens. Your efforts are likely to be rewarded several times over, and chances are you'll want to keep doing it. All it takes is a little creativity and a willingness to focus on your partner.

PART FOUR

Kissing

The mouth, including the lips and the tongue, contains one of the highest concentrations of nerves in our body, and as a sense organ, it is unique. Taking something into the mouth involves two senses—taste and touch. Because of the proximity of the nose and the close association between smell and taste, three senses are engaged when you kiss, and if you keep your eyes open, so is a fourth. We're hardwired to seek oral gratification before birth; images of thumb-sucking *in utero* are by now commonplace, and you don't have to be a Freudian to recognize that infants and toddlers are keen not only to ingest food but also to experience the world through their mouths.

As we get older and learn not to taste everything we find on the floor, this uninhibited orality wanes. We often eat meals in haste, at our desks, while reading, or while watching television. In doing so, we are cutting ourselves off from some of the most primal and plea-surable experiences that are available to us as human beings. This is unintended; we may think of ourselves as gourmets or connoisseurs, but most of us eat this way at least some of the time. Nevertheless, our mouths remain as sensitive as they ever were.

Similarly, many of us enjoyed extended make-out sessions when we were teenagers, and these sessions, which may or may not have gone any further than kissing, were often intensely erotic. Access to more direct sexual activity often leads to a decrease in kissing, as does the familiarity that comes with being in a long-term relationship. As a result, people often forget how powerful kissing can be, relegating it to mere preliminary status, making it something that is engaged in briefly (if at all) before moving on to what people often think of as the main event. A lot of pleasure gets lost in the process.

While we may not be able to recapture those teenage make-out sessions and all their feverish desire, we can pay more attention to kissing and make it a bigger part of our erotic repertoire. Kissing can be an art form, but it also has a more esoteric dimension. You may be surprised to discover that it played an important part in the most ancient Tantric rituals, as a transmission of energy, an alchemical process. It is a profoundly intimate act, sometimes more intimate than genital intercourse, because of the senses it engages and because our mouths are so close to our brains.

In addition, the mouth is a part of the body that has the capacity both to penetrate and to be penetrated. We can enter and be entered, thrust and be open to the thrusting. By becoming conscious of this potential in the mouth, kissing can function as an opportunity to explore the spectrum of gender that resides in each of us, regardless of our genitalia. Kissing is a very direct way of making what may seem to be an abstract concept into something very concrete.

Perhaps most importantly, kissing is fun. It is likely to make you feel more intimate and to bring you a lot of pleasure, if you allow it to. So explore kissing, kiss passionately, and savor the kisses.

CHAPTER TWENTY

Kiss for Ten Minutes

We have reminded you of what kissing was like back in your teenage years, but only in general terms. Now we want to make it personal, so try taking yourself back to that time, no matter how long ago it may have been. Remember the first kiss that did something special to you, the one that absolutely swept you away and opened you up to indescribable sensations. That kiss probably lasted a long time, more than a few minutes. You probably resisted the urge to come up for air and lost yourself completely in the experience. The whole session might have gone on for half an hour or more, and if you are like us, you were left breathless and elated.

That kiss was probably not foreplay. It was not likely to lead anywhere (even if you were hoping it would). Back then, if you are like most people, you were kissing for the sake of kissing.

Whether or not this was part of your adolescent experience, you can bring some of that youthfulness and wonder to your adult erotic life. Kissing may be one of the most neglected erotic experiences for long-term couples, but it is well worth your time and attention. The trick is to take yourself back to that mental state where you were kissing without any goal in mind, without thinking that it was a prelude to sex, and to kiss and keep on kissing.

By keep on kissing, we mean stay in a luscious lip-lock for at least ten minutes, while observing what happens to you. You may notice a change in the quality of your saliva, since it is commingling. Perhaps it will feel more fluid and taste sweeter. The idea that bodily fluids are intrinsically powerful substances is deeply embedded in the human psyche, and while people jokingly refer to kissing as "swapping spit," it is potentially an alchemical act that produces emotional changes.

You may find yourself getting incredibly turned on, wanting to rip your clothes off and tear into each other. This may happen very quickly, but we encourage you not to surrender to the urge, at least not the first few times you try this practice. Let yourself reawaken the sensations you experienced when kissing was not going to lead anywhere. See what it's like to limit the encounter to a ten-minute make-out session, with no touching of the breasts or genitals and no further sexual contact until the following day. Once you've experimented with this restriction for a while, you can see what it feels like to kiss for ten minutes as foreplay, or better yet, spend a week re-creating those years when there were limits on what kind of touching was allowed—none below the waist for the first couple of sessions, then a little genital touching through the clothes, next under the clothes, and then . . . at last . . . the main event.

You may be surprised by how much satisfaction you find in just kissing, and you are likely to drive each other wild by building the erotic energy gradually over the course of the week. Although there is no way to turn back the clock, and many of us would not want to be teenagers again, prolonged conscious kissing and tantalizing make-out sessions can help recapture some of that youthful passion and desire.

CHAPTER TWENTY-ONE

Give and Receive Kisses

People tend to engage in kissing (and most sexual activity for that matter) without giving much thought to what they are doing. This means that there are numerous unspoken assumptions. While this approach can be satisfactory, if people are well matched and reasonably well attuned to each other, it has its intrinsic limitations. For one thing, it means that we are groping for a good experience and are not doing all we can to ensure we will have one. More importantly, this way of engaging sexually never allows us to test our ability to give and receive pleasure. A more Tantric approach affords us the opportunity to explore the full spectrum of sensation.

Many Tantric meditative practices involve working with the interplay between external and internal stimuli. Remember that in Hindu Tantric cosmology, the universe is seen as an ongoing process of union between energy (which is conceptualized as the feminine principle) and consciousness (which is represented as masculine). On one level, Tantric sexual ritual is an attempt to re-enact this macrocosmic process on a microcosmic level. To go even deeper: this cosmic process of union between masculine and feminine polarities can be re-created internally by an individual practitioner, by means of visualization or a variety of other meditative techniques. Masculine and feminine in this context do not refer to our genitalia or to culturally constructed ideas about how "men" and "women" behave. We can, however, use our physical embodiment and our imaginations to enact and explore these energetic traits.

Kissing affords an opportunity to explore giving and receiving and also to play around with these polarities, by allowing yourself to be penetrated by your partner's tongue and then by doing the penetrating yourself. The experience of allowing oneself to be penetrated is very valuable for people who identify as male, especially those who have been well schooled in being aggressive and hard. By allowing someone to enter you, you are not only experiencing what it is like to be entered, you are deliberately taking on a role that is perceived as "feminine." Even though the Tantric polarities are energetic and not physiological, this act of playing around with and reversing gender roles is a way to make your sexuality broader, more fluid, more full spectrum. We think it is valuable for anyone, regardless of anatomy and/or identity, to experience as much of this spectrum as is possible.

We have already suggested that people often kiss back and forth without much awareness. This is partly because it is an unspoken expectation—just the way things are normally done—and partly because it can be uncomfortable to receive without giving back. We encourage you try a very different way of kissing.

Before you begin, decide who will be the kisser and who will be the kissed. If you are being kissed, simply allow your mouth to go soft, relax, be explored, and penetrated. Do not kiss back. This may be easier if you are lying on your back. Just allow yourself to have the experience, and see what you can notice in the process. If you are taking the active role, begin gently, just grazing the lips; bring your tongue into play but not too quickly; and don't penetrate your partner's mouth until you feel you have been invited (nonverbally) to do so.

After you have entered, probe tenderly. Experiment with deep and shallow penetration. Run your tongue along the teeth, both in front and behind. Pay attention to the different textures and tastes as you are kissing. See what it feels like to be tender, but also explore being more aggressive, using your tongue as if it were a phallus. Try alternating between the two styles.

Spend several minutes in your predetermined roles, and then reverse them. You may wish to combine this practice with the preceding one. Kiss for ten minutes, and reverse roles at approximately the five-minute mark, if you can keep track of the time.

CHAPTER TWENTY-TWO

Exchange Breath

We have written this book for the beginner. It is intended to be accessible for anyone who is curious about Tantra, and for those who want to learn a few techniques to enhance their sex lives. We chose the format to make the book user-friendly and to give you specific ways of giving erotic experiences more richness and depth, whether or not you have interest in delving into the tradition more deeply or exploring the many nonsexual aspects of Tantra. That said, some of the techniques we are sharing, while simple, are actually advanced, powerful, and may be somewhat obscure. Our teacher, Dr. Jonn Mumford, introduced us to the practice of exchanging breath. It is a traditional technique that he learned in India.

Exchanging breath is powerful on multiple levels. We have already discussed the meaning of the Sanskrit word *prana* and the importance of working with the breath in the Tantric and Yogic traditions. Remember that the word *prana* implies both breath and the energy that surrounds us, which we take in by breathing. Also remember that pranayama implies both regulation of the breath and regulation of the energy. More often than not, pranayama is a solo practice, designed to direct the flow of energy in your own body. This technique is pranayama for two, and it will affect you both physiologically and psychically.

The process is quite simple. All you have to do is maintain lip contact and exhale as your partner inhales. Next, your partner exhales as

Fig. 6: Exchanging breath during intercourse creates an energetic circuit

you inhale. Continue to exchange breaths in this manner for as long as you comfortably can. You may be surprised at the number of breaths you can exchange without coming up for air. There is no need to worry about lack of oxygen; our bodies absorb only a small percentage of the oxygen contained in each inhalation. When you start feeling that the oxygen has been depleted (this is actually due to the build-up of carbon dioxide, not a lack of oxygen), you can end the kiss and take a fresh inhalation. After that, you can take a break or return to exchanging breaths.

You can also try this technique during intercourse. It may take some practice, since coordination is a factor, but once you get accustomed to it, you are likely to have some very interesting experiences. From an energetic standpoint, you will be creating a closed circuit, since you are united above and below, and the energy of both your breath and your sex will be flowing back and forth between and through you.

If exchanging saliva is one of the most intimate of acts, exchanging the very air we depend on for life is even more profoundly so. In the context of intercourse, exchanging breath is likely to amp up your arousal and lead to orgasms that have a different kind of intensity, once you have developed the skills to do the practice when you are very turned on. Just remember to end the practice before either one of you starts to come, or you may end up with a chipped tooth (as we discovered). If you get lightheaded during sex, chances are it is because of the intimacy and charge of this erotic exchange. Whether you use the technique in intercourse, as foreplay, or just as a way to create more intimacy, this is a beautiful way to share the energy that literally keeps us alive.

CHAPTER TWENTY-THREE

Play with Cupid's Bow

In traditional Tantra, Yoga, and Ayurveda, it is believed that there is a set of psychic nerves, known as *nadis*, which exist within the body. This system of nadis is analogous to the more familiar system of meridians and points utilized in acupuncture and shiatsu. There is no need to become familiar with the entire system, or even to believe that the nadis have any physical reality. Indeed, Western science does not recognize the existence of meridians, acupuncture points, or nadis. Nevertheless, acupuncture and shiatsu can be effective treatments, so it seems that, whether or not the practitioners who developed these systems were literally right about the details, they were onto something significant. The same can be said about Leonardo da Vinci, whose drawing of a nerve connecting the breasts and the uterus was anatomically incorrect but still revealed an important phenomenon (the potential in some to experience orgasm through nipple stimulation alone). You may find something similar as you experiment with *Shanka Nadi* (literally, "conch channel"). Let your experience be your guide.

It is believed that the psychic nerve known as Shanka Nadi runs from the upper lip to the genitals. The traditional teaching is that it is only present in women, connecting the upper lip with the clitoris, but in our experience anatomy is no barrier to feeling the sensation. For those of us who are wired to feel it, the most important thing is self-awareness and attention. It is not a huge, intense, erotic charge, but more like a subtle tingle in the genitals.

In the traditional form of the practice it is believed that a man should suck a woman's upper lip while the woman simultaneously sucks on his lower lip. We have experimented with reversing these recommended roles and have found that we both can feel the sensation if we pay close attention.

Awareness of the erotic potential in this part of the body exists across cultures and finds some support in recent scientific research. The anatomical term for it, *philtrum*, means "love potion" in Latin, and it gives the lips their Cupid's bow shape. According to some systems of facial analysis, both Western and Chinese, a wide philtrum indicates that the person has sex appeal or a high sex drive.[21] Perhaps more surprisingly, a recent, peer-reviewed study published in *The Journal of Sexual Medicine* concludes that a prominent "tubercle of the upper lip" (the base of the philtrum) "was associated with greater odds . . . of ever having a vaginal orgasm."[22]

In acupuncture, there is a point on the philtrum that is used to revive patients who have fainted, are in shock, or have drowned.[23] It is believed that the point excites the central nervous system and causes an increase in blood pressure and blood flow to the brain, all of which can also have an impact on sexual arousal. Whether or not these claims, Eastern or Western, are true, their ubiquity is a testament to the power of this body part that is hiding in plain sight.

One final word on sucking on the upper lip (although it also applies to any technique in this book). Some time ago, we taught a couple about Shanka Nadi. We sent them home to experiment, and when they returned a few weeks later, they confessed that it felt a little bit awkward to kiss this way all the time and that they missed kissing the way they always had. We were stunned; we had not suggested they should give up their usual way of kissing. We assured them that sucking on the philtrum was something to add to their existing repertoire, not a replacement for it. So see what happens when you add this to the mix. You may find that it gives your kissing a little extra spice.

CHAPTER TWENTY-FOUR

Exchange Essences

This is a practice that some may find challenging and edgy, but one aspect of being a Tantric practitioner is the willingness to break taboos, and in the modern age, personal as opposed to cultural boundaries are probably the more interesting and valuable ones to cross. Nevertheless, this is a practice that you should only explore in the context of a fluid-bonded relationship. If safer sex is a consideration, you can substitute honey and exchange it in a kiss as a symbolic representation.

The earliest Tantric rituals involved the sharing and consumption of sexual fluids—semen, vaginal secretions, and menstrual blood. It was believed that this act was essential to effect the transmission of energy from one practitioner to another. David Gordon White did an outstanding job of explaining these beliefs and practices in *Kiss of the Yogini*, a scholarly work.[24] We discussed them from the modern practitioner's point of view in *The Essence of Tantric Sexuality*. This is an aspect of Tantra that gets little attention from most contemporary Western teachers, especially those who emphasize non-ejaculatory orgasms for men. Some describe female ejaculate as *amrita* (the nectar of immortality) in the context of making this type of orgasm a kind of Tantric *sine qua non*, but this is a distortion.[25]

We are fortunate that two of our teachers, Dr. Jonn Mumford and Dr. Rudolph Ballentine, did not avoid the subject of secretions. As with exchanging breath, the shared consumption of sexual fluids is an act that has profound implications. While we may live in a world that seems rational, science-based, and devoid of magic (these original Tantric practices had a magical dimension), we remain human, and the substances that are responsible for our very existence do not lose their power over us simply because we have been taught that they are mere chemical compounds. There are undoubtedly multiple reasons why the "cum shot" has become a staple in pornographic films, but one reason for it is the numinous quality of sexual fluids. This idea that bodily fluids contain some divine energy is embedded in the human psyche but often exists below the level of conscious awareness. It is present whether or not we believe in God, Goddess, God and Goddess, or any kind of magic.

By becoming conscious of this generally unconscious process, we can make use of it in ways that nurture us. By shedding our inhibitions and our discomfort with the messiness of sex, we become freer, more erotically engaged beings. The ancient Tantrics consumed sexual fluids because they believed that it was a way of obtaining power, and this is still true. If the thought of kissing after oral sex makes you uncomfortable, challenging yourself may prove to be a liberating and empowering experience. If it is something you already do, having an awareness of its implications may give it new meaning for you.

However you choose to approach it, this is perhaps the most intimate form of kissing of all. If you practice any form of ritual sex, incorporate it into your protocol. If ritual is not your thing, you can still think of this as a form of communion, a very direct and physical way of demonstrating your connection to each other.

PART FIVE
Awakening the Senses

The skillful lover knows that the most fulfilling encounters engage all the senses. At the same time, blocking one sense can make the others more acute, and exploring the interplay between sensory stimulation and sensory deprivation can be a powerful aphrodisiac.

It is interesting to note that both traditional Western and traditional Indian thought recognized five senses. The modern perspective is that there are several more: balance and acceleration, temperature, kinesthesia (closely related to but distinct from touch, the sense that enables you to touch your nose when your eyes are closed), pressure, and pain, to name a few. Nevertheless, people generally think in terms of the five senses, and in this section we will confine ourselves to smell, taste, sight, touch, and hearing. Of course, it is worthwhile for any aspiring Tantric practitioner to explore and experiment with the others as well.

In classical Tantra, the five senses are very important, and the texts often describe meditative practices that rely on one or more of them. In addition, the senses are closely connected to the five elements—earth, water, fire, air, and ether or space—that were seen as the building blocks of the universe in both Eastern and some Western occult traditions (Japanese and Chinese systems also recognize five elements). Tantric sexual ritual involves substances that represent each one of these elements. The connection between the senses and the elements is made explicit in the context of the chakra system (*chakra* means "wheel" in Sanskrit), a subject that is too complex and esoteric to explore in depth in this book. Our training with Dr. Mumford involved spending several weeks of practice and meditation on each chakra; this may seem like a long time, but it is brief by traditional standards.

There has been a great deal of nonsense written about the chakras, so if you are interested in learning more, be discerning and check into whether the source is rooted in the tradition. Studying the chakras is a great way to develop an understanding of your embodiment. You don't need to believe in their physical reality to work with them; they can function as tools for meditation and help you develop a more intimate awareness of your inner world.

Basically, the chakras are energetic centers that are believed to exist within the body; there are many ways of working with the chakra system in addition to techniques involving the senses and the elements. There are associated mantras, Sanskrit letters, *yantras* (geometric symbols), colors, animals, and deities. There are also variations among different schools as to how many chakras there are and where they are located. In the best-known system there are seven centers, and the senses are associated with the first five. These are the ones that relate to our physical embodiment:

Chakra	Location	Sense	Element
Root chakra	Pelvic floor	Smell	Earth
Second chakra	Pelvic bowl	Taste	Water
Third chakra	Solar plexus	Sight	Fire
Fourth chakra	Heart	Touch	Air
Fifth chakra	Throat	Hearing	Space or ether

The first and second chakras are the ones most directly associated with sexuality. Although we are visual creatures, smell is the most primal sense, often operating at a level below our conscious awareness. Taste and smell are interdependent.

There is great beauty and remarkable insight in the way the chakra system relates to our physiology and psychology. For example, the sensory avenue for the heart center is touch, and the genitals are the action organs for that center. If this awareness is somewhere in our minds every time we hold hands, not to mention every time we make love, we can recognize and perhaps understand how love and sex are deeply connected. We can also recognize that any consensual sexual act is an expression of love, at least at some level.

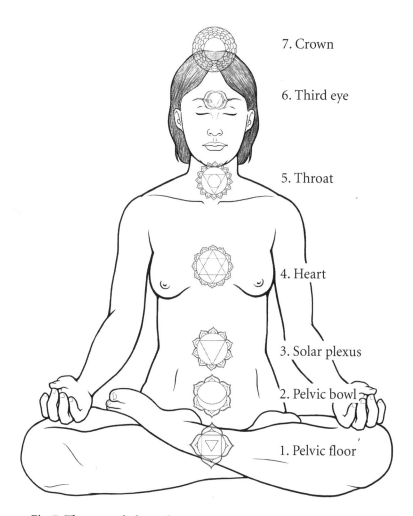

7. Crown

6. Third eye

5. Throat

4. Heart

3. Solar plexus

2. Pelvic bowl

1. Pelvic floor

Fig. 7: The seven chakras: the two uppermost, the third eye and crown, do not relate to the physical senses

The practices in this section are designed to help you tune in to your senses. Some of them are not sex tips per se, but becoming more conscious of your senses is likely to give you a more holistic understanding of sex. Awakening all the senses will open you up to the flow of erotic energy, and being mindful of their importance will help you orchestrate your encounters so that they can be multidimensional experiences.

CHAPTER TWENTY-FIVE

Smell:
The Most Primal Sense

The fact that smell is the sensory avenue for the root chakra is a testament to the insight of the Tantric and Yogic practitioners who described the chakra system. Smell is the most primal sense. It often affects us in ways we fail to perceive. In simple terms (and current research is revealing that the subject is considerably more complex), the sense of smell is governed by two systems: the main olfactory system and the accessory olfactory system.[26] Compared to many other mammals, the human sense of smell is rather weak, but it is still considerably more powerful than most of us realize.

The accessory olfactory system generally operates below the level of conscious awareness. It responds to pheromones and can enable people to recognize close blood relatives by smell alone. It is connected to the amygdala, a part of the brain that regulates fear and pain and processes emotion, and the hypothalamus, which links the nervous and endocrine systems and regulates body temperature, hunger, thirst, and circadian rhythms.

While visual cues are frequently the first trigger for sexual attraction, the accessory olfactory system probably plays a more critical role, once we've gone from seeing someone from across the room to talking at close range. All of this makes sense in evolutionary terms: distant odors, of fire or other threats, can get us ready to flee before we have consciously registered the danger. At close range, recognizing the scent of a close relative may limit our desire to engage in incest and thereby help us choose appropriate mates.[27]

The main olfactory system is considerably more complex, and it involves more areas of the brain, including not only the hypothalamus and the amygdala but also the orbitofrontal cortex, which regulates decision-making, among other things. Thus, it appears that smells processed through the main olfactory system have an impact both consciously and unconsciously. This aspect of the sensory avenue is also closely connected with the limbic system and the hippocampus. This means that smells can easily trigger memories, sometimes quite vivid ones. If you've ever taken an acting class and been exposed to sense memory as a technique, there's a good chance that the first sense you worked with was smell. The creators of method acting recognized something that has been known for centuries in Tantra and that modern science has validated: smell is the most unmediated of our senses, and we can use it to tap into hidden aspects of our psyches.

Whether or not you have taken a method acting class, you can begin to explore the power of this sense by doing a basic acting exercise. Perhaps the easiest way to do this is to choose a strong and somewhat unpleasant aroma—ammonia. This exercise is very simple: close your eyes, and breathe through your nose. Imagine that you are holding an open bottle of ammonia just under your nose. Breathe slowly and deliberately, calling the scent of ammonia to mind. Continue to do this until you have a visceral feeling that you are actually sniffing ammonia. This should not be difficult. Take a few more breaths, allowing yourself to experience the odor as completely as you can, and then open your eyes.

As a general rule, we like to focus on pleasurable sensations and guide people toward experiencing more joy in their lives. We apologize for the ammonia, but it is one of the easiest scents to evoke from memory, which makes it a good choice for a first try. Once you've successfully awakened your memory of that smell, you can try the same practice with something more pleasant: roses, spices, perfume, or sex.

Another way to explore your sense of smell and awaken this sensory avenue is to reverse the process. Instead of focusing on the memory of a scent, you can explore how certain scents may awaken a memory. This exercise requires two people and a blindfold. Have your partner choose five fragrant items, such as fresh fruits, flowers, pine needles, mint, or earth. Essential oils work too, but we encourage you to use the actual substances. Smell each item while blindfolded and take in the aroma without trying to identify it. The smell may evoke a memory, often a visual one, so if you're thinking, "That smell takes me back to Thanksgiving at my grandmother's when I was about six," you're on the right track. If you're thinking, "That smells like a mango," you're focusing on interpretation at the expense of the more primal elements that will come through if you can quiet your rational mind.

Now that you understand that smell is so primal and so central to the way you experience life, both in memory and in the moment, you can use the sense of smell to enrich your erotic life. It should not be difficult to find scents that you both find sexy. This is highly individual, but here are some of our favorites: basil, sandalwood, jasmine, vanilla, cinnamon, and bergamot. Once you have identified a few aromas that appeal to you, you can use them intentionally to create an environment that turns you on.

CHAPTER TWENTY-SIX

Taste: Where Our Sensory Experience of the World Begins

Taste and smell are closely related. It is no coincidence that the first and second chakras have taste and smell as their sensory avenues and are seen as being jointly responsible for sexuality. While all the senses are implicated in the human sexual response, smell and taste engage us perhaps more intimately and at a more primal level than the others. At the same time, taste is unique due to its dependence on other senses. When the ability to smell is impaired, so too is the ability to taste, and research has shown that wine drinkers (including connoisseurs) may have a difficult time distinguishing between red and white wines when blindfolded or when the wines are otherwise disguised.[28]

We have receptors for five kinds of taste: sweet, sour, bitter, salt, and *umami*—a Japanese word for the component of taste that makes us want to eat more.[29] It is sometimes translated as savory. The source of umami is glutamic acid, which is why monosodium glutamate is still widely used as a food additive. Umami is present in potato chips, Parmesan cheese, shiitake mushrooms, prosciutto, sugar snap peas, and tofu, as well as many other foods that make us eager to indulge.[30]

We can recognize all five of these tastes, either independently or in conjunction with each other, but we seldom taste something without engaging our other senses. The experience of eating or drinking involves not just taste and smell, but also our senses of touch, sight, texture (which is not quite the same as touch), temperature, and full-ness. In the context of most sexual activity, it is virtually impossible to engage the sense of taste without involving other senses simultane-ously, so we will ask you to take note of other sensory experiences as you explore the sense of taste.

When we lecture on the role of awareness in Tantric practice, we stress that one goal is to become facile with it, as opposed to striving for total awareness at all times. Developing facility with your aware-ness means that you can experience the full spectrum, from intense focus to complete withdrawal of attention, and have become skilled at choosing where along this spectrum you wish to be at any given moment. This has implications in sex as well, since one key to great lovemaking is the ability to be simultaneously attuned to your own state and the state of another, as well as the ability to shift your atten-tion as needed.

One of the many Tantric practices that helps develop this facil-ity is a technique the great Tantra teacher Daniel Odier calls "micro-practice." Micropractice involves engaging in everyday activities and pausing from time to time for a few seconds to experience whatever you are doing as completely as you can, and then returning to your habitual way of being. This technique can be applied to virtually any activity, and the act of focusing will always have a sensory dimension, but it is perhaps most easily employed and most dramatically effective when it involves taste.

To do this exercise, you will need three cups of water—one hot (but not too hot to drink), one cold, and one at room temperature. First take a sip from each of the cups, drinking as you would under normal conditions. Next pick up one of the cups, close your eyes, and take a sip and bring your full attention to it. Try to focus on the experience of drinking the water as completely as you can, feeling the water cross-ing your lips, moving over your tongue, down your throat, and into your digestive tract. Repeat the conscious sipping with the remaining cups. This activity engages multiple senses: taste, smell, touch, texture, temperature, kinesthesia, and abdominal fullness. Next, take a sip from each cup without focusing on the experience.

After you have completed the experiment, think about what it was like to take the casual sips of water, and compare that with the way it felt to drink consciously. See what differences you observe. Chances are they will be greater than you anticipated. Many Tantric practices are designed to bring our attention to the subtleties that are present in all experience. There is much pleasure to be had in the most mundane of activities, provided we develop the ability to notice it.

CHAPTER TWENTY-SEVEN

Sight: The Power
of the Erotic Gaze

Sighted human beings rely on this sense more than any other, and vision is arguably the most highly evolved of our sensory systems, even if our sight is very poor when compared to that of certain birds, raptors in particular. In humans, sight is the last sense to mature. It has been suggested that at birth we see upside down and continue to do so until the brain adjusts. This may be true for the first four months of infancy. After that time, infants react to images of inverted faces in the same way as adults. In general, visual acuity develops gradually during the first year of life.[31] The eye is one of the most complex organs in the body, and the interaction between the eye and the brain has been linked to the evolution of intelligence.

We receive most of our information about the world through our eyes. That includes information about the environment as a whole and about other people. More often than not, sexual attraction begins with a glance, and visual cues often let us know if the attraction is mutual. Similarly, we frequently recognize others' emotional states through visual input, even if that input is sometimes subliminal. Remember that one of the reasons the eye-gazing practice is so powerful lies in the fact that the left side of the face generally reveals more about a person's emotional state than the right (skilled poker players use this knowledge to their advantage).

Because sight is so important, it should come as no surprise that humans have been fascinated by erotic imagery since the days of cave paintings. In the West, ever since the rise of Christianity, erotic material of all kinds, but especially visual erotica, has generally been considered repulsive, harmful, degrading, and thoroughly profane. This attitude persists in the twenty-first century, perhaps most vividly in the efforts of some to define excessive viewing of pornography as an addiction. It is true that looking at erotica can be quite compelling and that some may do it to excess. At the same time, the evidence that this behavior is truly an addiction is ambiguous at best, and many of the advocates of this model base their opinions on thinly veiled religious beliefs.

By contrast, the attitude toward erotic imagery in India, Nepal, and Tibet was, at least historically, quite different. In Nepal, and to a lesser extent in India, it is not unusual to find the outer walls of temples decorated with very explicit erotic carvings. Tibetan Buddhist *thankas*, roughly equivalent to the religious icons of some Western traditions, frequently include depictions of deities in sexual union. Many of these images leave nothing to the imagination. While the purpose and meaning of this erotic religious art is sometimes the subject of scholarly debate, there can be no denying that the builders of these temples and the creators of these images understood the power of the erotic gaze. It also seems likely that they recognized that looking at sexually explicit imagery is a powerful experience, one that creates a change in consciousness, a kind of meditative and perhaps transcendent state.

There is a popular belief that men are more visual than women and therefore are more likely to be turned on by pornography. But some research indicates that the only real difference is whether people admit to being aroused by what they are seeing, and more women than men have been conditioned to find hardcore imagery distasteful.[32] Whether we admit it or not, few of us really observe what happens to us while viewing explicit images. Most people who enjoy erotic material simply use it as fuel for fantasy or as foreplay.

For this exercise, spend half an hour looking at erotic images. Choose whatever strikes your fancy, whether it is contemporary Internet porn, vintage photographs, or Indian, Japanese, or Chinese paintings. What-ever form of erotica you select, be sure you have enough material to spend half an hour viewing it. You can do this either alone or with a partner.

Instead of looking at this imagery for an overtly sexual purpose, you should allow yourself to be absorbed by looking at the images themselves. Do not masturbate or engage sexually; just look at the images and pay attention to the way you respond, whether it is with discomfort, arousal, boredom, some mixture of these, or any other reactions. Beyond that, think carefully about how viewing this mate-rial for a period of time, without a sexual agenda, has affected you, and whether you have experienced any changes in your conscious-ness. If you can experiment without judging, you are likely to discover a new way of seeing.

CHAPTER TWENTY-EIGHT

Touch: Open Up to New Sensations

You may recall that Dr. Mumford described Tantra as a tactile path. He has also suggested that one aim of Tantric sexual practice is to "transform the entire surface of the skin into a massive genital."[33] His statements highlight the centrality of touch within the Tantric tradition. This centrality is also evident in the association between touch and the heart chakra and in the role of the genitals, with their high concentration of touch receptors, as the action organ for the heart.

While other senses may be more complex, touch is perhaps the one that is most fundamental for our well-being. Long-term couples may find it difficult to gaze into each other's eyes or may no longer kiss, but as you know, we believe that literally losing touch is often the strongest indicator of serious relationship problems. Whether or not you have a partner, it is important to find ways to be touched and frequently. We have already suggested that getting regular massages is one way to ensure that this basic need is met. It is also good to find a social circle in which touching is embraced.

We'll give you some exercises for exploring this sense. They should be fun and perhaps surprising.

The first two exercises we'll offer are to be done with a partner. If you are doing this alone, then try the third option. In the first two, you'll use your fingers and the nose. The nose is important because it is reflexively connected to the genitals. Like the genitals, it contains erectile tissue; the thickness of the nasal mucosa ebbs and flows in conjunction with the menstrual cycle; and there is a condition formerly called "honeymoon sinusitis," which involves nasal swelling caused by prolonged arousal. For similar reasons, Viagra and other such drugs are contraindicated for some people with respiratory problems.

The exercises involve two illusions: one is known as the Pinocchio Effect and the other is called Aristotle's Illusion. We are sharing both because the Pinocchio Effect only works in approximately 50 percent of the population, and we want to be sure you experience something. For our purposes, these exercises are significant not because they show how unreliable our senses can be, but because they illustrate the potential for discovering delightful new sensations, even in seemingly mundane activities. Also, from the Tantric perspective, a subtle

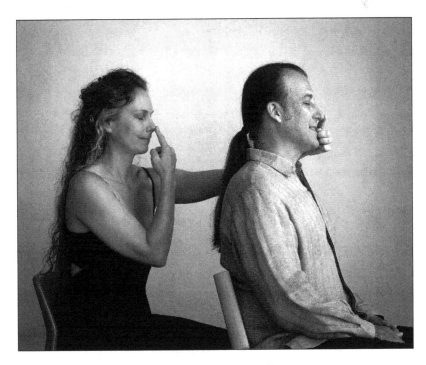

Fig. 8: The Pinocchio Effect

Fig. 9: Aristotle's Illusion

surprise can create an opening, a shift in consciousness that gives us a glimpse of infinite possibility.

To experience the Pinocchio Effect, take two chairs and face them in the same direction, placing one in front of the other. Sit behind your partner. Close your eyes. Place your dominant index finger on your partner's nose (you may need to be guided). Place your other index finger on your own nose. Gently tap and stroke your partner's nose and your own simultaneously. Try to keep the movements synchronized and equal in intensity. Continue for about thirty seconds. Notice any sensations. Take a break, and reverse roles.

For Aristotle's Illusion, sit facing each other. You should each cross the index and middle fingers of one hand, close your eyes, and simultaneously touch the tips of each other's noses with both fingertips. Again, notice what you experience. If you are alone, you can try it with any small round object—a pea or a marble.

There is yet another illusion we'd like you to consider, and this is not an exercise. Perhaps you have experienced it during particularly intense or intimate sexual encounters. You may have lost the ability to tell where your body ends and where your lover's begins. If so, you know how our physical senses can deceive us.

While we may not always be able to rely on our senses to tell us what is "real," we can always observe what we are experiencing. We can also always be open to new sensations and find surprise and delight in the simplest of tactile experiences.

CHAPTER TWENTY-NINE

Hearing: Alter Your Consciousness with Sound

In Tantric anatomy, the sense of hearing is associated with the throat chakra, and the action organ for that chakra is the voice, which reflects the understanding that speaking and hearing are closely connected. It is believed that the throat chakra is the last of the physical centers and that it is the gateway to mental and spiritual realms.

Tantra is primarily an oral tradition, and there is a great emphasis on the passage of teachings from "mouth to ear." This is also implicit in the word *Upanishad* (which refers to a group of sacred Hindu texts). *Upanishad* can be translated as "ear-whispered teachings." All of this implies that hearing and speaking are powerful ways of connecting ourselves with the sacred dimension in life.

There are a number of traditional Tantric meditations that involve hearing. This is due, in part, to the nature of sound. Sounds are considerably more variable than other sensory cues: they can be soft or loud, distant or close, steady or wavering. This makes it possible to work with them in very interesting ways. The *Vijnanabhairava Tantra*, a pre-eminent Kashmiri Tantric text and one of the greatest meditation manuals ever written, describes one such technique: "If one listens with undivided attention to the sounds of stringed and other musical instruments which on account of their (uninterrupted) succession are prolonged, he will, at the end, be absorbed in the ether of consciousness."[34] In this meditation, the practitioner listens to the sound, follows it as it begins to fade, and then stays in the silence, with the music still resonating mentally.

Hearing is also interesting because it functions in two ways. Airborne sounds produce vibrations that are received by the ear, converted into nerve impulses, and processed by the brain. Underwater sounds are heard by bone conduction, a fact that has significant implications in terms of the connection between hearing and the voice and with regard to the use of mantras.

Mantras are sounds that function both to focus the mind and to produce changes in physiology and consciousness. One of the best known and most powerful of all mantras is the familiar syllable Om (ॐ). It is said that Om is the only mantra that anyone ever needs, and if you try chanting it aloud for fifteen minutes, you may learn why.

The correct way to chant it is to place one-third of the emphasis on the "O" sound and two-thirds on the "mmm." The power of the vibration is in the "mmm," because it is transmitted through the skull into the sphenoid sinus and from there into the sphenoid saddle, which houses the pituitary gland. This stimulation of the pituitary contributes to the change in consciousness that most people feel after just a few repetitions of the mantra.

When we chant Om aloud, the vibrations reach our ears through both the bone and the air, which diffuses the power of the mantra to some degree, although it still remains quite effective. If we take measures to ensure that the vibration is only transmitted through the bones, the power of the chanting is magnified. Here are two interesting and easy ways to experience this.

As a solo practice, you can lie in the bathtub, submerge your ears, and chant, ensuring that the sound waves are only transmitted through the bones. Doing this for a few minutes should produce an altered state of consciousness.

It is more interesting and more intense to try the partnered approach. Stand facing each other and place your heads side by side so that your right ears are aligned. Press your heads together so that your ears are touching and sealed off. Cover your partner's other ear with

Fig. 10: Chanting Om in unison with ears together
can create harmony and connection

your right hand, and have your partner do the same to you. This will
block out most, if not all, the airborne sound waves. Next chant Om
together several times, while making sure you have sealed off the ear
openings as fully as you can. Feel the vibrations and hear the combined
sounds reverberating through your head. You may notice some surprising sensations and hear a variety of overtones. In addition to being
interesting and consciousness-altering, this can be a very effective way
of, literally, harmonizing with each other.

CHAPTER THIRTY

The Full Spectrum:
Engage All the Senses
in Lovemaking

The best sex usually engages all of the senses, but there is nothing wrong with those quickies that only involve one or two. We certainly enjoy them. That said, working intentionally with the senses—whether by activating them all or selectively impeding one or more—is a great way to bring new textures to your lovemaking.

Hindu rituals generally are structured so as to affect all the senses, and the classical Tantric sexual ritual is no exception. The practitioners' senses are engaged through chanting, the burning of incense, the lighting of butter lamps, the sharing of food and drink, and sex in the presence of others. There is no need for you to re-create that ritual (or engage in sex in a group setting) in order to incorporate the basic approach into your lovemaking, at least from time to time. This is not about elaborate ceremonialism, but it does require some care and attention. Many of us did something similar when first dating or when trying to seduce someone new. There is no right or wrong way to devise an encounter that is designed to excite all the senses. Every individual's version will be slightly different; so instead of telling you what to do, we'll offer some general guidelines for what to consider.

For starters, you'll want to set aside enough time to savor the experience. To awaken the sense of smell, you can use incense or essential oils. If you are allergic, aromatic foods are a good substitute.

To activate the sense of taste be sure to include foods that are both light and flavorful. For some, the taste of mangos is sexually evocative; for others it may be oysters. The latter are nice, not so much for their purported aphrodisiac quality, but because they so strongly evoke the water element.

For sight, you can dress provocatively and feast your eyes on each other, put some beautiful flowers in the room (which may also engage the sense of smell), or look at erotic material that you both find appealing.

Touch (and taste) can be engaged by feeding each other and also by the texture of your clothing. For the more adventurous, spanking or another form of impact play can be very effective. (This suggestion may seem surprising to some, but Tantra is non-moral, and there is even a passage in the *Vijnanabhairava Tantra* that mentions piercing as a gateway to mystical experiences.)

For hearing, use whatever music you like to set the mood. Sing, if you find each other's voices pleasing, or whisper lovingly to each other.

If you're not currently in a relationship, you can set up a self-pleasuring session and follow the same general guidelines. It can be delightful to seduce and make love to yourself. Few of us take sufficient time to do this.

A more bare-bones approach to working with all the senses does not require any outside props, food, or elaborate planning beyond being sure that you have bathed. What it does require is mindfulness. As you engage sexually, focus on what's happening and how your senses are involved.

Notice your lover's smell and taste as you draw near and kiss or engage in oral sex. Keep the lights on, but not too brightly, and keep your eyes open. Pay attention to how the sight of your beloved affects you as you interact. Observe how you respond to touch, and what your touch does to your partner. Notice how different the sensations are when you make contact with your hands, with your body, and with your genitals. Finally, and for some this is the most challenging, make noise while you make love. Even if it feels a little artificial at first, sounds have a remarkable way of building energy and creating an erotic crescendo, so let go and be loud. There's another benefit to making sounds deliberately. Doing so will ensure that you are breathing well and deeply. This will bring more energy to the experience.

All of these elements are no doubt familiar to you, but it never ceases to amaze us how readily people forget to include them, either due to inhibition or because they've lost the habit. People have a tendency to believe that sex should be spontaneous and that everything will go smoothly and wonderfully if the chemistry is there and the other person is "right." This may happen from time to time, but it has more to do with luck than with chemistry or the quality of the match. If you approach sex with consciousness, intention, and a deep awareness of the role the senses play, your encounters are likely to be more consistently delightful.

PART SIX

Erotic Trigger Points

Most people are familiar with at least some of the body's erogenous zones, but even so, they often tend to limit their focus to the three or four most obvious ones—the lips, breasts, genitals, and possibly the anus (if they're somewhat adventurous). It's ironic and more than a little sad that some become less skillful as lovers as they grow more experienced. When people are young, sex is new and fascinating, and intercourse may not be an option. During this stage, they're likely to spend hours making out, caressing each other, and exploring their bodies. We've already touched on this in our discussion of kissing, but it really applies to all aspects of sexual experience. Again, there is something to be said for recapturing some of what it was like to be sixteen.

The exploratory enthusiasm we may have had as teenagers often wanes, not only because it is easier to have access to sex as we grow older but also because we may be in a long-term relationship that has an established routine. We may take our partners for granted in bed, just as we may fail to pay attention to them in other ways. In many cases, people forget just how delightful sexual exploration can be. The fact is that the entire body (not to mention the mind) can function as an erogenous zone, if you are open to the sensation, and the person stimulating you is attuned and giving.

You're probably familiar with some of these erotic trigger points, but if you're over twenty-one, there's a good chance you haven't made the most of them in years. Some of the others may not have been areas you focused on (or knew about) as a teenager, but they can provide you with very intense erotic pleasure if stimulated at the right time and in the right way.

We learned a system of working with the erogenous zones that is based on a traditional South Indian approach from Dr. Mumford, who introduced it to the West nearly forty years ago. This system, called the *Kama Marmas* (pleasure points), is an exquisite road map for building arousal. While it is a wonderful way to enhance lovemaking, it takes some time and dedication to master, and it's most useful in the context of extended sex. If your time is limited, you can focus on one or two of the erotic trigger points that are likely to drive your partner wild, in very short order. Some of these areas are part of the system, and others are not. If you wish to become more intimately familiar with the Kama Marmas, they are discussed in detail in our first book, *The Essence of Tantric Sexuality*, and depicted in *Advanced Tantric Sex Secrets*, one of our instructional DVDs.

Regardless of how much time you have and how many erogenous zones you stimulate, it's always best to build a good deal of arousal before engaging in genital or anal contact, and you can use the first four trigger points (and any other erogenous zones you like) to get things started. Then you can move to the more sensitive areas.

CHAPTER THIRTY-ONE

Nape of the Neck

The slang term *necking*, meaning "prolonged kissing" or "making out," dates back to the early nineteenth century and was widely used until at least the 1960s. Although the term is somewhat archaic today, there is still a fairly common understanding that kissing someone on the neck is a way of communicating sexual desire, of saying, "I want you." According to a dating website: "If a guy kisses you on the neck, it [means] that he cannot wait to get more 'intimate' with you."[35] While we're not familiar with the origins of that piece of folk wisdom, it's certainly true for us.

It's also just one of many beliefs about the neck that highlight the erotic power that resides in this part of the body. A bite on the neck is part of the mating ritual in cats and other members of the animal kingdom. The nape of the neck is very sensitive to more subtle contact, so there's no need to be as aggressive as a wildcat, although getting bitten in this area can be a huge turn-on too, especially if you're already highly aroused. The line between pleasure and pain (or between painful pleasure and painful pain) varies a great deal from person to person, so if you're going to get rough, you have to be careful not to cross it.

But we're getting ahead of ourselves. The nape of the neck is our favorite area to touch when we want to transition from our everyday activities into making love. In fact, we often call it the transition point. Approaching your lover from behind and kissing the back of the neck is a great way to signal your interest, and touching the neck is relaxing and soothing, intimate and sensual. It stirs the sexual response but in a gentle, comforting way.

Sexual excitement is really a mix of arousal and relaxation. The sympathetic nervous system and the parasympathetic nervous system have to function in balance and harmony for sex to work. Caressing the nape of the neck activates both systems.

Try gently gathering up your beloved's hair and running your fingertips along the hairline. Next, stroke gently from the hairline down to the top of the shoulders. Add a few light kisses and a whisper or two in the ear. If you do, you'll be simultaneously stimulating another erogenous zone. This is almost sure to put anyone in the mood.

Hot breath on the back of the neck can send chills down the spine. You can also lick a small area and then blow gently on it. The effect of the evaporating saliva is cooling and calming, with a subtle erotic edge. When you're both a bit more turned on, you can try nibbling, biting gently, and gathering your beloved's hair in your hand and giving it a tug.

To return to the animal kingdom for a moment, most pets enjoy a good scratch on the neck. They often roll over and offer up their bellies in a display of pleasure. If you caress, kiss, and stimulate the nape of your partner's neck, you may get a similar reaction.

CHAPTER THIRTY-TWO

Armpits

The armpits might not spring immediately to mind as an erogenous zone. Some people do fetishize them, but the vast majority of us associate the armpits with hygiene or the lack thereof. They are the home of odors and hair and must be kept clean at all costs.

Both the odors and the presence of hair point to the erotic potential that lies hidden in the armpit. While the armpits are not orifices, the hair evokes the genitals, and frottage (rubbing) in a well-lubricated armpit can be very exciting (and safe) for both participants, evoking intercourse without any actual penetration. It was a popular fetish in the nineteenth and early twentieth centuries.

The armpits are also key perspiration points, where your personal scent and pheromones are highly concentrated. From this perspective, deodorants are a mixed blessing. Although they can mask the unpleasant smell of stale sweat, they also interfere with one of the most important and subtle components of attraction.

As we've discussed, smell is our most primal sense. It plays a very significant and underappreciated role in attraction and sexual excitement. By nuzzling into your lover's armpit, you're engaging that primal sense and turning yourself on in the process. People vary a great deal in terms of their sensitivity. For some, strong smells are intoxicating; for others, it may be best to nuzzle shortly after bathing. Whether you prefer your partner freshly bathed or a little sweaty, this is a great way build each other's arousal.

Fig. 11: Early-twentieth-century French postcard depicting frottage

The armpits are replete with nerves. In fact, one of the most lethal strike points in martial arts is located deep within the armpit (many erogenous zones double as strike points in martial arts, exactly because they are so sensitive). It's also possible to open your left nostril by applying pressure to your right armpit, and vice versa. This is an ancient Yogic method for controlling brain function and inducing either a relaxed or an active energized state at will.

When one nostril is open, the opposite brain hemisphere is dominant, so breathing through the right nostril suggests that you are in a more active, intellectually sharp mode of operating. Breathing through the left means you are more likely to be relaxed, reflective, and receptive. You may find that after particularly good sex, both nostrils are open. This is a sign that your brain hemispheres and sympathetic and parasympathetic nervous systems are in balance.

In addition to frottage and nuzzling, we find licking gently is the most effective way to engage this erogenous zone. You can begin at the front, and lick along the edge of the pectoral muscle, gradually working your way toward the center. Another tantalizing approach is to combine licking and gentle exhalations in a circular motion, moving from the outer edges toward the center.

Some people find hairy armpits very sexy and others do not, just as they do with the genital area. Questions of taste are highly individual, regardless of cultural norms, so you'll have to discover what appeals to you, something that can change over time. Whatever your personal preferences, this is a very responsive and often neglected part of the body.

CHAPTER THIRTY-THREE

Inside of the Elbow

This is another very sensitive area that often gets overlooked. In fact, like the armpit, it is one of the zones Dr. Mumford omitted when he adapted the Kama Marmas for the Western world. In a few of our classes, we've been asked why we don't mention the inside of the elbow (we do talk about the backs of the knees, which are analogous), so it seems that some people remain consciously aware of how responsive this area can be, even in adulthood. We've both had lovers who got very turned on just by a few kisses on the inside of the elbow, but for many people, the sensitivity is quite subtle.

Like the armpit, this is a strike point in the martial arts, and if you've had blood drawn badly by an inept doctor or nurse, you know just how tender this area can be. We're not bringing up the martial arts and medical professionals because we want you to think about violence, pain, and suffering but rather to illustrate that these zones are both vulnerable and erogenous. The skin is thin, so the nerves and blood vessels are very close to the surface. Remember, if an area is sensitive to pain, chances are it will be sensitive to pleasure, too.

In the case of the elbow, the nerve involved is the ulnar nerve, which is the largest unprotected nerve in the body (and the one responsible for the sensitivity of the "funny bone"). Interestingly, the ulnar nerve connects to the little finger, which is also an erogenous zone. We'll have more to say about the little fingers in chapter 41.

The inside of the elbow is a particularly nice erogenous zone because you can fondle it discretely almost anywhere and at almost any time. As with kissing the nape of the neck, it's a great way to send the message "I want you," and it is a little less obvious when you are out in public. Gentle stroking of this zone with one or two fingers can be quite tantalizing. If you're in a more private setting, a deep tongue kiss in the crook of the arm will create an erotic charge. Licking, blowing, and stroking, or any combination thereof, can all be effective. The sensations you experience may be subtle ones, but becoming skilled at Tantric lovemaking involves honing your ability to recognize these less obvious pleasures.

CHAPTER THIRTY-FOUR
Achilles Tendon

Few people think of the Achilles tendon as an erogenous zone, but acupuncturists have long contended that placing needles in certain points near that tendon can relieve menstrual cramps, induce labor, and treat impotence. Traditional Indian healing systems also recognized the sensitivity in this area and its connection to sexual response. Knowledge of this sensitivity exists in the West as well, for the most part in a different form. We have known since Homer's era that the Achilles heel is a vulnerable spot, but we don't generally think about it in sexual terms, at least not consciously. High-heeled shoes accentuate the elongation of this part of the body, something that happens during orgasm, but that association generally registers on an unconscious level.

Unlike the other areas we've discussed, this is a specific trigger point, not an erogenous zone, although the area between the ankle and the calf does fall into the latter category. When we first learned about it from Dr. Mumford, we were skeptical about its potential for producing a response. Then we tried it ourselves, observed how it worked for others, and were convinced.

While we were shooting *Tantric Sexual Massage for Lovers*, we shared this point with the couple we were teaching on camera, and one of them had a spontaneous and totally unexpected orgasm when the right pressure was applied to the right spot. Although she was very sexually self-aware and experienced, she was completely surprised by

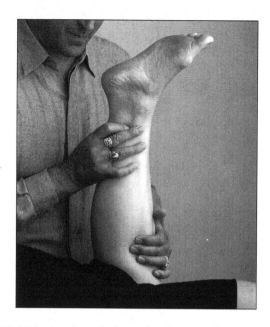

Fig. 12: Massage along the lower leg, between the bone and the Achilles tendon, to find the trigger point

her response. While some may not be as lucky as she was, this is a little-known area that is full of erotic potential.

The exact trigger point can be a little tricky to find. It's just above the ankle. The best way to locate it is to have the receiver lie face down. Massage up the leg from behind the ankle joint, and apply pressure on both sides of the area, between the tendon and the bone. Be sure not to press into the tendon itself.

Initially, the person receiving may only notice a tingling in the leg. This is a sign you are on or near the spot. It may take some experimenting to locate it exactly. Once you do, the sensation is likely to go up the leg to the genitals.

Start gently, and be careful; some people can tolerate a lot of pressure, while others require a softer touch. Sensitivity in this area can vary and is often related to the menstrual cycle, so it is important to ask for feedback. Pay attention to visual and aural cues, and bear in mind that the response can be different every time. As is so often the case, sudden hip movements, sighs, and soft moans are good signs.

CHAPTER THIRTY-FIVE

Coccyx

The coccyx, or tailbone, is at the very base of the spine—the place where those chills you sent down from your beloved's neck landed. In the Tantric tradition, it is said we have a gland at the base of the spine and that our life-force energy resides in that gland. For now, we'll explain this in physiological terms. This is the location of the *coccygeal plexus*, a grouping of nerves that serve the genitals and lower pelvis. These nerves shape your sexual response.

We've found that stimulating this area actually impacts the entire nervous system, and the more aroused you are, the more interesting your response is likely to be. If you've ever fallen hard and banged your tailbone, you know that the sensations are intense and can impact your entire body. The force of the blow may even have left you momentarily paralyzed. In fact, many Tantrics believe that such an incident can lead to a life-changing, mystical experience.

Tuck a finger into the very top of the cleft between the buttocks, and apply gentle pressure. Although the area is usually more responsive in higher states of excitement, some people find that a mere touch to this part of the body elicits arousal. You can also try tapping lightly anywhere from the very base of the tailbone to the top of the buttocks or even a little higher. The lower back is also replete with nerves that connect directly with the genitals and that play a part in the orgasmic response.

When tapping, you can either use your fingertips or the edges of your hands. This light drumming will send vibrations and nerve impulses into the genital region. You can also slide your finger up and down, between the tip of the tailbone and the top of the cleft. And of course, kissing, licking, and/or blowing (which are gentler and less direct) are very erotic. This can be a turn-on at any stage of your sensual play.

If you want to be a little more ambitious, tuck a finger into the cleft, and locate the tip of the spine. Maintain contact and apply steady pressure while vibrating your finger. This will send tingling sensations through your lover's body. Try using this method during intercourse, as it is likely to provide additional, indirect genital stimulation. The nerve impulses will also travel up and down the spine and may be felt throughout the body.

Unlike the nape of the neck, the very tip of the spine is not an area to jump to right away. That's usually somewhat too intense for most of us, but once your partner is turned on, you can go there. It doesn't really take much. You can begin by stroking the nape of the neck for a few minutes, and transition to kissing. After a few minutes, you can sneak a finger down the back and vibrate the tailbone before moving on to more overtly sexual interaction. It's a great way to electrify the entire body with just one finger.

CHAPTER THIRTY-SIX

Nipples

Now we're moving on to more obvious and familiar trigger points. They relate directly to the ever-popular breasts and genitals. They may be obvious and familiar, but that doesn't mean we know all there is to know about them. There's a lot more pleasure to be gained if you arouse them deliberately, understand what you're doing, and learn a couple of new tricks.

Although the nipples are well-known erogenous zones, people often touch them mechanically and without paying much attention. Some may rely exclusively on grabbing the entire breast (not a recommended seduction strategy), pinching the nipples, or sucking or biting them. When we teach about nipple stimulation, we sometimes find it difficult to get students to slow down, focus, and be methodical.

If people approached the breasts with the devotion we'd like them to bring to oral sex, they might come to equal the genitals as an erotic destination. While society makes a fetish of the breast, the attraction tends to be visual, which is one reason surgical augmentation is so popular. Some associate large breasts with sexual responsiveness, even though it is not uncommon for people to lose some degree of sensitivity, and sometimes most of it, after having the surgery. Recent improvements in surgical techniques have reduced but not eliminated the potential for nerve damage. There are certainly circumstances in which surgery is appropriate, but the potentially negative impact on sexual pleasure is frequently overlooked.

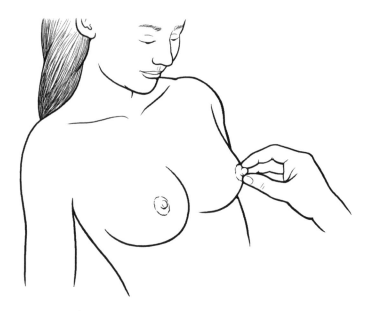

Fig. 13: Stimulate both the nipple and the areola

Indeed, many people can have orgasms through nipple stimulation alone, and while it is something of a taboo to say so, it is not uncommon for nursing mothers to orgasm while breastfeeding. A smaller number of male-bodied people also have the ability to experience orgasm in response to breast play, and most people enjoy nipple stimulation regardless of anatomy; however, not everyone does.

You can use your hands, mouth, lips, and teeth in a variety of ways. Try licking the nipples and then blowing on them, as you did with the nape of the neck. The nipples contain erectile tissue, so the cooling effect is likely to make them hard. You can also try pinching, rolling, and tugging. Moisten your fingers with saliva first, and use your thumb and index and middle fingers to tease the areolas and nipples. Since the nipples have more nerves than the areolas, sliding from areola to nipple again and again can build and intensify arousal. For some lucky people, this alone will be enough to produce an orgasm.

People's breasts and nipples vary a lot in terms of size, shape, and responsiveness. Pregnancy, nursing, and the menstrual cycle can also influence sensitivity, as can your level of sexual arousal. For some, the nipples are almost always very responsive and can function as "on buttons." Others, by contrast, don't like their nipples touched until they are highly aroused.

Some people enjoy light touch that others might find irritating. Some like to have their nipples stimulated in ways that may seem painful to others. Thus, it is important for the receiver to communicate clearly and for the giver to pay attention to the response. Experiment with different types and styles of touching, and you're likely to come up with one or two that work. Take some time and linger on the breasts; they're not just a way station as you head for the genitals. They're a wonderful source of pleasure in and of themselves, so enjoy them to the fullest.

CHAPTER THIRTY-SEVEN

Above the Pubic Bone

We each stumbled upon this zone independently, in the course of our own erotic explorations. Interestingly enough, the traditional symbol for the second chakra, the sex center, is a crescent moon, the tips of which touch the crests of the hips and the base of which sits on the pubic bone. We weren't thinking about the chakra system when we started playing around with this point, but as it happens, we were stimulating it in a very direct way. Even if you think the chakra system is a bunch of mystical nonsense, we strongly suspect that you'll enjoy stimulating this point.

The best way to find it is during self-pleasuring, and once you discover the right spot, try applying pressure to it just as you are about to come. This is likely to intensify your orgasm. Just be sure you have emptied your bladder first; otherwise you may experience some discomfort.

Placing a hand above the pubic bone and pressing in a little and then downwards, so that you are reaching under the bone slightly, makes indirect contact with the internal parts of the genitals, and especially the G-spot and prostate. It may take some time for you to find the right angle and figure out how much pressure to apply, since we're all built somewhat differently, but with a little practice you'll find the spot and deduce how strongly you should press. Once you do, you can explore applying pressure earlier in your self-pleasuring.

*Fig. 14: Press in and down to find the
erotic trigger point near the pubic bone*

After you have found the location and know what works for you, you can direct your partner to the exact point and provide guidance.

Unlike some of the other trigger points, this area is not close to the surface of the body. Thus many people can tolerate a lot of pressure, especially if they have strong abdominal muscles. Most people don't like having direct pressure applied to the pubic bone itself, which can be painful. But once your partner gets behind the bone, your response should be quite different.

It can be very enjoyable to add direct genital stimulation—oral or manual. When you are really turned on, applying more pressure can take you even higher. One of our favorite ways to work with this zone is to combine it with internal G-spot or prostate massage. This combination of internal sensation and external pressure produces orgasms that can be stunning in their intensity.

CHAPTER THIRTY-EIGHT

Perineum

In strict anatomical terms, the perineum encompasses the entire pelvic floor, from just above the external genitals to the coccyx, but if you're like most people, you probably define it differently. In common parlance, the perineum, popularly known as the *taint* or *gooch*, is the area between the anus and the genitals, and we are using perineum in that popular sense.

In the early stages of working with the PC muscles, people learn to contract and release them, focusing on the entire pelvic region. In order to learn the more advanced Tantric techniques, it is necessary to start isolating different parts of this musculature. If you want to start refining your PC muscle skills, you can begin by trying to isolate the taint when you pulse. Just imagine that there's a tiny point midway between your anus and your genitals and that you can draw it up into your body. If you focus on this point and apply intention and attention to your pulses, you should be able to become skilled at controlling the movement of your muscles.

There is a tendency to think about the genitals in a very limited way. For instance, the penis is visible, so people often don't realize that there are two additional inches inside the body. If you're worried about size (and you shouldn't be), you can now think of yourself as being more generously endowed. Similarly, people seldom think beyond the labia, vagina, and head of the clitoris. The truth is that the whole pelvic area is suffused with nerves and erectile tissue. The clitoris, in particular, has a wishbone shape, and while the head is the most sensitive part, you can stimulate the legs by rubbing or applying pressure between the inner and outer labia. There's no need to limit yourself to exploring the most obvious parts of your partner's sexual anatomy. You can discover new sources of pleasure by thinking outside the box.

Like all the erogenous zones, the perineum is very sensitive and rich in nerve endings. It's a great place to experiment with anal eroticism, if you're not quite ready to be more direct; and even if you are, the fact that you are experienced is no reason to ignore this area. It can be very titillating to massage the perineum gently with one or two well-lubricated fingers, or you can use your breath, lips, and tongue.

If your lover is in a high state of arousal, you may want to provide a more intense form of stimulation. If so, you can vibrate the perineum with your fist. If your partner has a prostate gland the vibrations will go directly to it (more about that in the next chapter) and to those hidden inches of the penis. It's wonderfully arousing and considerably less intense than internal stimulation, so it can be a great precursor to anal penetration. The same principles apply if your partner has female genitalia and no prostate. The sensation will reach the legs of the clitoris and the oft-neglected erectile tissue between the anus and the floor of the vagina. Applying a vibrator to this area also works very well.

It's great to spend some time here before moving to more direct genital or anal contact. If you do, chances are you'll drive your lover wild with anticipation.

CHAPTER THIRTY-NINE

Prostate Gland

While sexual orientation and gender identity have become more fluid, especially among younger people, a large segment of society still associates enjoying anal stimulation, and especially anal penetration, with homosexuality and humiliation. This attitude is embedded in our language. "Shove it up your ass" and "Go take it in the ass" (to translate the French and Italian versions of the expression) are insulting phrases with homophobic overtones that are intended to express extreme displeasure.

Not only is there the misguided notion that enjoying anal play has something to do with sexual orientation, but this is also a part of the body that we tend to think of as unclean. This is a somewhat more rational attitude than having concerns about orientation, but issues of hygiene can be easily addressed. There's also the unfortunate fact that most people with a prostate first experience anal penetration in the context of a physical examination. Unless you have a medical fetish, chances are you don't find a doctor's office very sexy. Not only that, the lube is usually cold; the whole process is abrupt and unpleasant; and your pleasure is the last thing on the doctor's mind.

Anal pleasure can be an acquired taste. It can take some time to learn to enjoy the sensation. This may be true even if you are intellectually aware that the anus and prostate are highly sensitive erogenous zones. For some who start experimenting with receiving prostate massage, it can be mildly unpleasant at first and may take several sessions before the brain recognizes the experience as a pleasurable one. For many, it can become a favorite sexual treat.

There are sex toys available for massaging the prostate, but we think the best way is to use a well-lubricated finger, especially when you are just starting out. Using a finger enables the person giving the massage to tune in to the receiver's response a little more closely. Toys can interfere with your ability to control the stimulation, although they can be great once you're more experienced, and they may be useful in the context of self-pleasuring.

It is always a good idea for the giver to wear gloves, especially if you're a little concerned about being clean, but more importantly for reasons of safety. Anal tissue is delicate, and wearing gloves will

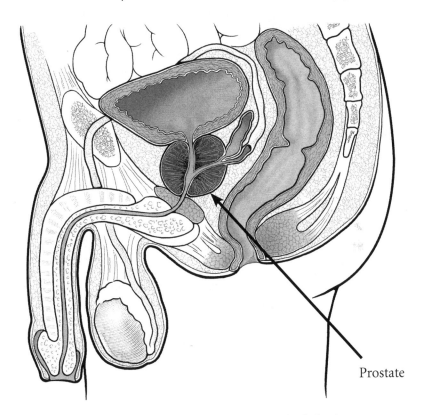

Prostate

Fig. 15: The prostate feels like a walnut-sized gland.
It can be digitally stimulated through the anus.

protect you both. If you have long fingernails, you can pad the area around them with cotton balls to provide cushioning. As an aside, if you're serious about sexual pleasure in general, it is best to keep your nails short and well groomed. The smallest sharp edge can turn an otherwise exciting encounter into a disaster, so don't be a slave to fashion; instead, make pleasing your partner a priority.

The prostate feels like a walnut-sized gland (although it's actually larger). It is located at the base of the penis, and it produces much of the ejaculatory fluid. You'll find it between a half and a full finger length inside the anus, toward the front of the body. It's surrounded by and covered with many of the nerves that are responsible for erection, so it's very sensitive. In esoteric Tantric anatomy, it's believed to be a direct trigger point for the second chakra, the sex center.

It's always best to build a great deal of arousal before attempting to penetrate the anus. In many instances, you can allow the receiver to set the pace of penetration and invite you in, by opening up and bearing down slightly. Once you're inside and have located the prostate (don't worry if you can't find it on the first few tries), rest your finger on the prostate and remain motionless at first. When your partner is ready, you can begin to massage it with a come-hither gesture. Be sure to continue stimulating the penis—manually or orally. The orgasm that this produces is likely to be intense and exquisite.

CHAPTER FORTY

G-spot

There's a lot of mythology around the G-spot, which is not a spot at all but an area of erectile tissue that surrounds the female urethra. It is the anatomical analogue of the prostate gland and similarly is a trigger point for the second chakra. While the G-spot was named for Dr. Ernst Gräfenberg, who "discovered" it in 1950, it was well known in ancient India and was discussed in some of the classical Indian sex manuals.[36]

The known Tantric texts, which discuss the ritual uses of sexual fluids generally, don't stress the G-spot or the fluid it can produce. Nevertheless, some contemporary Tantra teachers treat ejaculatory G-spot orgasms as the ultimate in Tantric practice and the source of sexual healing. We have a somewhat different perspective and prefer not to think of one kind of sexual experience as superior to all others. We've known people who can ejaculate in response to G-spot stimulation and feel little or no pleasure when it happens, and we've known very seasoned sexual adventurers who have never ejaculated at all and still have fulfilling sex lives.

We're all different, and there's no one-size-fits-all approach to sexual responsiveness. As with any other zone, G-spot massage may or may not be pleasurable for you, and there's nothing wrong with either reaction. It's just yours, but be aware that as with prostate massage, this can be an acquired taste.

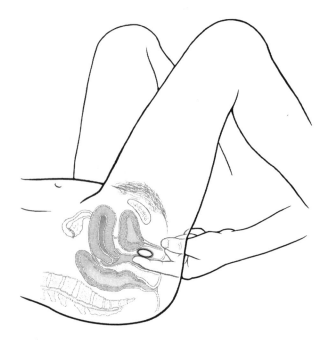

Fig. 16: The G-spot is located within the upper front wall of the vagina between two-thirds and a full finger-length inside

For many, the biggest mystery about the G-spot is its location. It's at the front of the vagina, in the upper portion, behind the pubic bone. As with the prostate, it's easiest to find with a finger. If you insert one or two fingers when your lover is highly aroused (in multi-orgasmic people, it's a good idea to do this after one or more clitoral orgasms), you're likely to feel a ridge of slightly rough, engorged tissue approximately two-thirds to a full finger length inside. That's the so-called G-spot. The best way to massage it is to use the same come-hither gesture that we described for the prostate gland. It can be helpful to keep the palm of the hand in contact with the clitoris, and as we have already suggested, incorporating the trigger point above the pubic bone is a great way to intensify the response.

Sometimes the G-spot responds to a lot of pressure. Sometimes the response is more energetic than physical, and just resting your finger on it is all that's needed to produce an orgasm. The G-spot can also be very tender, especially when the receiver is not excited enough.

You don't want to press the urethra into the pubic bone, which is likely to happen if the surrounding erectile tissue is not engorged. Sensitivity can also vary a great deal during different phases of the menstrual cycle.

Don't forget to communicate clearly, carefully, and kindly, so that the experience is as pleasurable as possible for both of you. As with prostate massage, it may take some time before someone who is new to the experience can identify the sensations as pleasurable. This is a matter of forging new neural pathways, so if there is a little discomfort at first, don't attach any meaning to the sensations; just observe without judging. The way you perceive the feelings may very well shift. Of course, if you experience real pain, it may be a sign that you are not sufficiently aroused or that this is not a good practice for you at this point in your life.

It can be very helpful to empty your bladder before you start. Many people inhibit the ejaculatory response because they confuse it with the need to go to the bathroom. You'll feel freer if that's not a concern.

Finally, if you want to learn to ejaculate, it's very important to be well hydrated, so be sure to drink a good deal of water during the day of your session. While having ejaculatory G-spot orgasms is not a goal in Tantra, many people love having them, and they can be a huge turn-on for the giver as well. G-spot stimulation is certainly a treasured part of our sexual repertoire.

PART SEVEN
Enhancing Oral Sex

Oral sex can be a profoundly mystical and spiritual act. Some cultures have recognized this for millennia. Unfortunately, for those of us in the English-speaking world, oral sex gets a bad name. It is often depicted as an act of domination and humiliation. Expressions like "Blow me" and "Eat me" are nothing if not hostile and negative. Of course, all sorts of sexual and sexually related anatomical terms are used in similar ways, but "It sucks" is one of the most common and socially accepted of all these expressions. Unlike most other similar phrases, it doesn't get censored.

At the same time, oral sex doesn't qualify as sex in the minds of some. Whatever his motives, when Bill Clinton denied having "sexual relations" with Monica Lewinsky, he was not far out of line with a culture in which many people think that "eatin' ain't cheatin'," as the saying goes.

Although attitudes toward oral sex have changed considerably since the time when it was criminal in many states (some of these laws are still on the books but have been declared unconstitutional), it remains a taboo, and a source of discomfort, for many. A poll conducted in the late 1990s found that only 32 percent of women performed fellatio, oral sex on a penis, for pleasure, while the remainder did so out of obligation.[37] A more recent study showed that among young people, ages 18–26, a majority of men enjoyed performing oral sex, an attitude shared by only a minority of women.[38] Giving (as well as receiving) oral sex can be immensely pleasurable for virtually anyone, and we can only assume that if cultural attitudes were different, vast majorities of both young women and men would acknowledge enjoying it.

A subtler but still widespread and somewhat negative attitude toward oral sex is that it is appropriate only as foreplay, not as an end in itself. This seems to be the view of the Catholic Church, which deems nonprocreative sex to be sinful. According to one Catholic writer, oral sex is only acceptable if it is used to help produce simultaneous orgasms through genital intercourse.[39]

This is a terribly benighted view of sexual activity, and treating simultaneous orgasm as the right kind of sex, the goal to which all should aspire, is a prescription for sexual disappointment and dissatisfaction. Some other Catholic sources have a more generous attitude toward oral sex and treat it as acceptable foreplay, if done with moderation (whatever that means).[40] As we see it, not only is oral sex great as foreplay; it is also a delightful form of sexual activity in its own right.

If you want to play around with cultural ideas about oral sex, by all means feel free to do so. Incorporating domination and humiliation into an erotic interaction can be a real turn-on for some people, but it is important to be aware of what you are doing. There is a difference between really believing that performing oral sex degrades you and playing a role to spice things up. The former is allowing your state of mind to be governed by the sex-negative messages we have all received, and the latter is using your state of mind (and those sex-negative messages) to empower yourself and to increase your pleasure.

As we have already discussed, it is important to be mindful of safer-sex protocols and to make informed decisions; if you are fluid-bonded (have made an agreement to share sexual fluids), the exchange can be a profoundly intimate act, with mystical overtones. If you are not and are using barriers, you have a number of options; you can replace the sexual fluids with symbolic substances or visualize the energetic exchange. Whichever you choose, oral sex can be an act of worship and reverence when approached with the right attitude. As we wrote in *The Essence of Tantric Sexuality*, when performing oral sex "you are either on your knees or prone and are physically attached to a living altar."[41] If you carry this awareness with you at some level, you will have the capacity to recognize the transcendent in what is often considered a shameful act.

Oral sex can also be incredibly exciting, for both giver and receiver. For some, receiving it is the source of the most intense orgasms, and there are fortunate individuals who can experience orgasm by giving it. Even for those who are not so blessed, it can still be intensely arousing to bring a lover to ecstasy. Perhaps more importantly, the mouth is very sensitive, and our earliest pleasures are oral. With or without orgasm, if you can truly focus while giving oral sex, it is easy to lose yourself in the ecstatic experience.

In this section, we'll share some effective ways to make oral sex even more pleasurable and some visualizations that should give you access to its transcendent potential.

CHAPTER FORTY-ONE

Use the Aural to Enhance the Oral

In our discussion of hearing, we touched briefly on the sensitivity of the ears, but there is more to be said on this subject. While the ears are not composed of erectile tissue, they may flush red when we are sexually excited or nervous. This reaction is governed by the sympathetic nervous system, which is responsible for arousal and the fight-or-flight instinct. At the same time, evidence suggests that direct stimulation of the ears activates the parasympathetic nervous system, which produces feelings of relaxation.

It is well known that the ear is an erogenous zone (it actually contains two erogenous zones, the lobes and the openings). Because the ears are linked to both the sympathetic and parasympathetic nervous systems, we suspect that stimulating the ears serves to harmonize these two systems, which must be operating in balance if you are to become aroused and experience a satisfying orgasm.

If the sympathetic nervous system is dominant, you may have a premature ejaculation, find it difficult to quiet your mind sufficiently to become aroused, or be so tense that orgasm is not possible. Conversely, if the parasympathetic nervous system is dominant, you may be too lethargic to respond. Incorporating the ears in your sexual play may help balance these two systems and improve your erotic response.

Fig. 17: Inserting moistened pinkies into your partner's ears during oral sex creates two energetic circuits and is a delightful way to guide the pace of stimulation

The little finger is also an erogenous zone. The little fingers are recognized as being very sensitive in cultures around the world. They are considered the psychic fingers in Western occultism, and in some Japanese traditions, it is believed they are connected with the heart. In our system, both the ear openings and the little fingers are considered tertiary zones because they are either unresponsive or averse to touch unless you are in a high state of arousal. If you can remember getting a "wet willy" (wet fingers in the ears) when you were in elementary school, you'll understand how important it is to be absorbed in your sexual encounter before trying this technique. The way you reacted to this childhood prank may also help illustrate how contact with the ears can affect both components of your nervous system.

While we discussed the erogenous zones in some detail in *The Essence of Tantric Sexuality*, we did not really address the concept of creating energetic circuits. This particular practice is a very effective way of doing just that. By bringing together your little fingers and your partner's ears, you are linking two tertiary erogenous zones. In our system, the mouth and the genitals are considered primary erogenous zones, so in this process you are creating two separate sets of energetic connections between your bodies. There's no need to subscribe to any esoteric beliefs about energy or to do anything special; the awareness that you are creating these circuits should generate a change in the experience regardless of what you believe about it.

The actual technique is very simple. If you are receiving oral sex, moisten the tips of your little fingers with saliva and gently insert them into your partner's ears. Be sure you've agreed on doing this in advance. Giving someone a surprise wet willy is sure to kill the mood, but if it's expected, it can be an erotic intensifier for you both.

As the receiver, you can be a little dominant and guide the giver's movements, setting a pace that works for you. The giver on the other hand is subject to some limited sensory deprivation, especially if the eyes are closed as well. This facilitates becoming completely absorbed in the activity. Due to the stimulation of the parasympathetic nervous system that placing the fingers in the ears produces, the giver may go into a trance-like, blissful state, one in which everything but the pure experience of orally worshipping the receiver disappears.

CHAPTER FORTY-TWO

Oral G-spot

Like many Sanskrit words, *mudra* has more than one meaning. It can refer to a form of parched grain that is consumed during the Tantric sexual ritual, but more importantly for our purposes, it means a gesture that creates psychological and/or physiological changes. Some of these changes can be quite dramatic; for example, we've been initiated into mudras that direct the breath to different parts of the lungs. Mudras are not exclusively hand gestures. They may be invisible, because they are being performed inside the body.

Khechari mudra (literally, "the gesture of wandering in space") is one such invisible mudra; it is one of the most difficult to learn and is considered by many to be the most potent of all. It involves stretching the tongue until it can be inserted behind the uvula (the bulbous tissue that dangles down at the back of the soft palate, protecting the opening of the pharyngeal cavity). Some practitioners actually cut the frenulum of the tongue (the piece of tissue that connects the tongue to the bottom of the mouth) so that they can perform it.

This is a symbolically sexual act, evoking intercourse between the tongue and the throat. It involves mastery of the gag reflex; it triggers the taste buds and produces a sweetness that is said to be that of *amrita*, the nectar of immortality. It is also a tool for focusing awareness and regulating the breath.

Because it is so difficult to perform khechari mudra, a modified version involving what we call the oral G-spot is taught in many Tantric and Yogic schools. In Taoism, this is known as the "fire point." The oral G-spot is not, strictly speaking, an analogue to the more renowned vaginal G-spot that can be stimulated to trigger ejaculation. It is, however, a highly innervated location in the mouth with an erotic potential that tends to be overlooked.

It is located toward the back of the roof of the mouth, about two-thirds of the way between the front teeth and the point where the soft and hard palates meet. To find it, probe the roof of your mouth with your tongue. If you apply pressure, you will find a spot that is quite sensitive. Its location is just below the part of the skull through which the olfactory cilia dangle into the nasal passages, separated from the air by a thin membrane.

Humans are hardwired to be oral for a number of reasons, and the sensitivity of this particular part of the mouth is one component of the hardwiring. Breastfeeding brings repeated pressure to the roof of the mouth, and thumb sucking also stimulates this point. Use your thumb and try tapping gently backward from the front teeth toward the soft palate, while making note of the sensations. Experiment with tapping on both sides and down the midline. Don't go so far back that you trigger the gag reflex. You may feel a vibration that runs up into your nose, creating a sense of tingling and fullness.

For some people, focusing on this point and working with it can make it easier to become orgasmic while performing fellatio. Thinking energetically and using your imagination are very helpful in this context. You can imagine an electrical current flowing through your lover's genitals and filling your cranial cavity. Keep your focus on drawing the energy up into your skull through the oral G-spot and on the physical sensations you are experiencing. We can't guarantee that using this technique will make you orally orgasmic, but it is sure to add something new to your experience of oral sex.

If you're at all skeptical about the power of this spot, consider this. Some years ago we did an interview on Playboy Radio. The hosts of the show were Christy Canyon and Ginger Lynn, two very prominent former porn stars. When the subject of the oral G-spot came up, they had their doubts that it even existed. We were quite insistent about it, and as it happened, they had a vibrator in the studio, and being sexually creative people, they came up with the idea of applying the vibrator to the spot. They were both thrilled and amused by this new discovery and by the sensations. Try it yourself, starting at a low intensity, and see what happens.

CHAPTER FORTY-THREE

Become a Human Vibrator

Unlike many of the terms that are used to describe oral sex, *hummer* doesn't have overtly negative implications. Although we haven't been able to ascertain the origin of the term, we'd like to believe it relates to this technique and refers to a particularly effective way of performing oral sex, a way of turning your mouth into a vibrator. It seems that the term *hummer* is usually applied to fellatio, but it's just as valid for cunnilingus, stimulating the clitoris and vulva with the mouth and tongue; in fact, the method we prefer is easier to practice during cunnilingus. For fellatio, intention is more important than pronunciation.

Being vocal during sex is a powerful aphrodisiac. It is also very valuable to make sounds while going down on your lover, and by making sounds, we don't mean faking orgasmic moans. In general terms, it is best to find sounds that are a genuine expression of your enjoyment. It can be easy to be so focused on giving pleasure that you neglect what can be a powerfully erotic enhancer.

When the person giving oral sex makes humming sounds, the vibrations are transmitted directly into the body of the receiver. These vibrations influence both the receiver, who feels them in the genitals, and the giver, who feels them in the skull. This technique is in some ways similar to using a vibrator, but a human being is producing the sounds and vibrations, and that human being is intent on sharing pleasure. Thus, the effect can be considerably more subtle and complex.

These vibrations may not be as intense as mechanically generated ones, but an energetic exchange is taking place, something that can lead to a very different kind of experience. Not only is the giver focused on giving pleasure, but the receiver's response and the cues it provides through several sensory avenues also create a feedback loop that will, ideally, take you both into very high states of arousal.

We have discussed chanting Om and given you a direct experience of its power in the context of exploring the sense of hearing (Part Five, chapter 29). Chanting this syllable during oral sex has a similar but directly sexual impact. If you are performing fellatio, you probably won't be able (and shouldn't try) to make the "O" sound, so just focus on the "mmm," while repeating the "O" part of the mantra mentally.

We'd like to examine in more detail the significance of this seemingly meaningless syllable about which so much has been said and written. The symbol for Om predates written Sanskrit, and the syllable is often referred to as the primordial sound—the vibration that emerged at the birth of the universe and that persists as the pulse of creation. Tantric sexual rituals involve reenacting this ongoing process of creation. The symbol itself is suggestive of sexual union—ॐ.

The part of the symbol that resembles the number three evokes the *yoni*, or feminine aspect, while the curvy line that also resembles a tail symbolizes the *lingam*, or masculine aspect. By chanting the syllable, you are symbolically uniting your own inner masculine and feminine aspects, in addition to producing the physiological impacts we discussed in the chapter on hearing.

Om is actually composed of three distinct sounds compressed into one syllable, and it is sometimes transliterated AUM (Ah—Oo—Mm). The first two sounds combine to produce the "O." These three letters have profound symbolic significance. They represent past, present, and future, and thus evoke the timeless states that can be experienced during lovemaking.

They also symbolize the Hindu trinity—Brahma, Vishnu, and Shiva —who represent respectively generation, operation, and destruction: GOD (although we prefer to say generation, operation, and transformation). From this perspective, God need not be imagined as an anthropomorphic being but instead as the process of existence. This kind of theism strikes us as being far more sensible than believing that God is a creator who is not a part of creation. Om also symbolizes the life cycle, which is of course dependent on sexuality. At a minimum, these are useful metaphors, and even if the metaphors don't work for you, the physiological effects of chanting the syllable are real.

Remember that when chanting Om, you should divide it up so that the "O" sound comprises the first third of the chant and the "mmm" the second two-thirds. We have already discussed how chanting in this manner affects the pituitary gland and resonates through the skull. We should add that it also vibrates the oral G-spot. The crescent and dot that appear above the symbol indicate the extended "mmm" sound. The dot is called the *anuswara*, which is sometimes translated as "little heaven." By chanting Om correctly, you are creating a heaven in your own cranium; chanting it during oral sex will take both of you there.

CHAPTER FORTY-FOUR

Pleasure Your Partner Inside and Out

By now you should have been able to locate the G-spot and the prostate, and your explorations have probably brought you much pleasure. As we have already pointed out, the G-spot and prostate gland are anatomical analogues that developed differently *in utero*. As you may recall, from an esoteric perspective they are trigger points for the second chakra or sex center. It is certainly true that for most people, direct stimulation of these areas is intensely erotic, provided the person receiving the stimulation has been sufficiently aroused in advance. Combining oral sex with prostate or G-spot massage can transform the intensely erotic into the explosive.

Before going any further, we want to reiterate something that probably cannot be restated often enough. If you are hesitant about having your prostate massaged, you are missing out on a lot of potential pleasure. You are also missing out on experiencing what is probably the closest approximation to what sex is like for a person with female genitalia. Of course, the approximation is somewhat crude, but it is one of many ways you can play around with your anatomy and with your perceptions about gender polarities. Similarly, this is an opportunity for people who don't have penises to do the penetrating. Developing the broadest possible spectrum of bodily experience and knowledge affords us the opportunity to become freer human beings, less constricted by socially determined roles.

A few other general reminders may be of value at this point. The best way to stimulate both the prostate and the G-spot is by making a come-hither gesture with your middle finger. Some receivers may prefer two fingers, especially for G-spot massage, in which case the middle and index fingers are probably best. Review our advice about fingernail care and gloves in Part Six, chapter 39. We recommend gloves for all prostate massages and for those who are not fluid-bonded.

Be sure to spend a good deal of time on the external parts of the genitals first. The more arousal you can build, the more receptive and responsive the receiver will be. For some, a few clitoral orgasms can serve as foreplay. Also be sure to use a lot of lube, especially for prostate massage, since the anus doesn't produce any lubrication of its own. It's a good idea to keep towels on hand, as this can be one of the messier forms of sexual play.

Giving oral sex and internal massage simultaneously may be a bit of a challenge at first because it requires hand-mouth coordination. This kind of multitasking is probably less familiar and a little more awkward than trying to coordinate both hands during manual-digital stimulation. If you are the receiver, be sure to give both encouragement and helpful feedback. Also, you may find that touching yourself on another part of your body adds a third point that will give you even more pleasure. Playing with your own nipples can work well, and so can applying pressure just above the pubic bone, the trigger point we described in Part Six, chapter 37.

Once you've become adept at combining oral sex and digital stimulation, and it really shouldn't take long, try chanting Om while doing so. If you become skilled at this form of multitasking, you are likely to take your partner to new heights of ecstasy.

CHAPTER FORTY-FIVE

Imagine Your Way to a New Dimension

As you may recall, the word *prana* refers not only to breath but also to the energy that pervades the universe. The study of prana is quite complex, and there are various subtypes, but in the context of visualization, all you need to do is think of it as something invisible that surrounds you and that you can take in through your nose and mouth. Oral sex is a particularly fertile arena for incorporating visualization because it is so primal and because we do in fact take in energy through our mouths, at the very least in the form of food.

It is important to distinguish between visualization and sexual fantasy. Both are imaginative acts, but the purposes are quite different. We can use fantasy to arouse or distract ourselves, and it certainly has a place in sexual activity, whether solo or partnered. Sexual fantasies usually involve calling images to mind, and understanding that fantasy is a form of visualization will help you become more skilled at painting mental pictures; however, the purpose of visualizing in this particular context is not to build arousal or to help you reach orgasm. The purpose is to make the sexual encounter richer and more psychologically layered.

Visualization is also a tool for increasing the mutuality of your lovemaking. As we have already observed, from the Tantric viewpoint, all sexual activity, even very casual sex, engages the heart. From a Western perspective, this can be understood as being due in part to the post-coital release of oxytocin. Thus, every sexual encounter involves some degree of bonding between (or among) partners, although some go to great lengths to resist, reject, or ignore this element. When both partners visualize that they are exchanging energy, the bonding process is strengthened. Each is facilitating the other through a creative, imaginative act.

The process of doing this is simple, and you have already had a taste of it if you tried visualizing in conjunction with exploring the oral G-spot. The receiver should picture drawing prana in through the top of the head and down and out through the genitals. The giver imagines sucking this energy in through the receiver's genitals.

People have different capacities for and ways of visualizing. For some, imagining colored light (gold is usually best) or wisps of smoke or mist can be the most effective way to see prana in the mind's eye.

Fig. 18: Basic visualization of an energetic circuit during oral sex

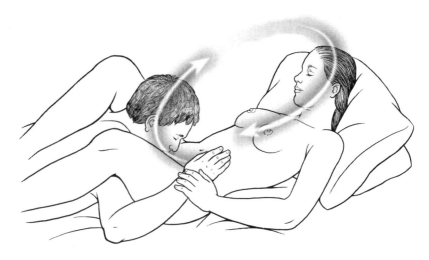

Fig. 19: Advanced visualization of an energetic circuit during oral sex

Others may prefer to imagine the tingling sensation of an electrical current or a sound vibration. If you find yourself struggling, you can simply tell yourself mentally that you are drawing in and exchanging energy.

Once you have mastered the basics of this visualization, you may want to elaborate on it by imagining that the energetic exchange is a closed circuit rather than an open one. In this more advanced version, the giver should imagine that the energy drawn in through the mouth is flowing out the top of the head, and the receiver should visualize that current entering through the crown. The current flows in a circular motion from receiver's genitals to giver's mouth, from crown to crown, and back out through the genitals. By visualizing this exchange, you are establishing yourselves as two bodies in energetic communion, wrapped in a flow that is potentially endless. If you can truly surrender to this imaginative experience, you are likely to feel a deep sense of connection.

Oral sex is powerful and primal. In some ways performing it evokes infancy and therefore can take the giver into a deeply focused, altered state of consciousness. For the receiver, it is potentially the most pleasurable form of sexual contact. At the very least, bringing consciousness to your oral encounters is likely to deepen your bond. It may even give you a glimpse of sex at its most transcendent.

PART EIGHT

*Sex Positions:
A Tantric Twist*

In many, perhaps most, human cultures, the sky is considered masculine, while the earth is figured as feminine. This is true throughout the Indo-European world, although there have been countervailing belief systems, of which Tantra is one. According to the Hindu Tantric model, Shiva is inert consciousness, a corpse (*shava* in Sanskrit) without Shakti, the feminine, energizing principle. For this reason, Tantric art often depicts the Goddess, in one or another of her many forms, astride and being penetrated by a dormant, corpselike Shiva.

The origins of this Tantric concept may be ancient, much older than the tradition itself. These beliefs seem to have existed in India for millennia, alongside the more conventional Sky Father/Earth Mother dichotomy, although it is also possible that the early Tantrics were engaging in antinomianism (going against moral or religious law) and deliberately setting orthodoxy on its head. In any event, this reversal of the dominant paradigm found formal expression in the earliest Tantric sex rituals, in which ferocious female sky deities known as *Yoginis*, who were reputed to feed on human flesh, would possess the bodies of female practitioners and transmit their power to males known as *Siddhas* (perfected ones) or *Viras* (heroes). As we have already discussed, the exchange of power depended on the sharing of sexual fluids.[42]

As centuries passed, Tantra evolved; the emphasis on spirit possession waned; and both the sexual ritual and philosophy grew more spiritualized and congruent with more conventional Hindu beliefs. At the same time, Hinduism absorbed many Tantric concepts. Notwithstanding this evolution, Tantric ideas about masculine and feminine aspects did not change. These ideas continued to be expressed in art and in sexual ritual, in which female superior positions were central because they both reversed the conventional view of masculine sky and feminine earth and enacted the feminine/energy–masculine/consciousness polarity.[43]

Members of the GLBTQ (Gay, Lesbian, Bisexual, Transgender, Queer) community sometimes criticize Tantra, and especially Western sexual Tantra, for being heteronormative (defining heterosexual activity as standard, thereby marginalizing other forms of sexual expression). There is considerable merit to these objections, especially with regard to Tantra's contemporary manifestations; it is also true that no known Tantric texts deal with same-sex activities and that heterosexuality and strict gender definitions have characterized the tradition throughout most of its history. At the same time, as one of our teachers, Dr. Rudy Ballentine, pointed out to us, many Tantric texts have yet to be translated or published and many others were destroyed during the Islamic invasions of India, so it is quite possible that some such texts were composed, and may even still exist. It is certainly the case that South Asian temple art depicts virtually every form of human sexual activity imaginable.

Regardless of this historical dimension, it bears repeating: the energetic principles that are figured as feminine and masculine in Tantra have nothing to do with anatomy or with gender roles as they exist in twenty-first-century society. The Tantric tradition is not a dogmatic one, and Tantric fundamentalism is an oxymoron. From this perspective, neither sexual orientation nor gender identity is an impediment to practicing Tantra. If the concepts and symbolism appeal to you, all it takes is a little imagination.

With this understanding, we can re-envision "female superior" positions as "person being penetrated" positions. The person penetrating is assuming the inert, masculine role, and the person being penetrated is assuming the energizing, feminine one. If you choose to visualize yourself as becoming one or the other gender, this can be immensely valuable, especially if you are cis-gendered (your gender as defined at birth, anatomy, and self-identification all match) and heterosexual. This reversal of roles and identities can be an important exploration.

In more practical terms, if the person who is being penetrated takes control and sets the pace, that person is apt to experience more pleasure, which will then cycle back to the penetrator. For people with female genitalia, being on top is far more efficient in terms of both clitoral and G-spot stimulation, and for people with male genitalia, being on the bottom and letting the person being penetrated set the pace makes it easier to regulate the ejaculatory response and prolong arousal. Thus, the traditional Tantric sex positions are more than just symbolic expressions; they can also make sex a more pleasurable experience for most of us.

For the sake of convenience and good style, we will refer to the person penetrating as *Shiva* and the person being penetrated as *Shakti* and use masculine pronouns for Shiva and feminine pronouns for Shakti.

CHAPTER FORTY-SIX

Pull Yourselves Together: Yab Yum

Yab Yum is the quintessential Tantric sexual position. It is probably familiar to many, as it is frequently depicted in both Hindu and especially Tibetan Buddhist art. In Yab Yum, the partners are face to face, with Shakti astride Shiva. In the classical version, Shiva sits in the full lotus posture, with Shakti on his lap, her legs wrapped around him. If you are unable to sit this way, and many of us aren't, it is perfectly fine to sit on a pillow in either half lotus, a posture that is technically known *as Ardhapadmasana*, or just cross-legged (*Sukhasana*). If this too is uncomfortable, you can sit on the edge of a bed or a chair, with Shakti astride. This is known as *Yoni Asana*, or womb pose. All of these variations provide the same basic benefits.

This is one of the most intimate sex positions because your bodies are close together, aligned, and face to face, which makes it great for eye-gazing. You maintain the position by embracing, so you are literally pulling yourselves together. This also allows you to move your hands along your partner's body, either to stimulate other erogenous zones or to make contact with the various chakras—small of the back (sex center), mid-back (solar plexus), center of the back (heart), nape of the neck (throat), and back of the head (third eye). You can also make slow upward sweeps and imagine that you are directing energy up the spine.

Fig. 20: Yab Yum

Yab Yum allows for alternating between active, movement-based sex and a slow, meditative style of lovemaking. It allows you to sit in stillness and experience the quiet beauty of uniting your body with that of your beloved. Sex is about more than thrusting, and sitting in Yab Yum is one of the easiest ways to develop an appreciation for this more subtle kind of pleasure. If the sexual energy begins to diminish, you can pulse your PC muscles to reignite it. Exchanging pulses, which is sometimes known as "the secret language," can be a particularly sensual way to do to this.

The classical Tantric sex positions allow Shakti to set the pace. This makes being penetrated an active rather than a passive or receptive role. If you have female genitalia, this can result in a more pleasurable and orgasmic experience. Because of the angles involved, many people find that Yab Yum is the easiest position in which to experience G-spot orgasms through genital intercourse. This is by no means true for everyone, and digital stimulation (as opposed to intercourse) is by far the most effective method for triggering the ejaculatory response.

If you are embodying Shakti and being anally penetrated, setting the pace can give you a feeling of control and therefore more enjoyment. It can be difficult for some to relax the sphincter when atop. This varies from individual to individual, so for certain people, Yab Yum may not be optimal for receiving anal sex.

Finally, sitting Yab Yum, without direct genital engagement and either clothed or naked, can be a very effective way to create intimacy. It makes eye-gazing even more potent, since your bodies are in contact and aligned. In this position, your breathing and your emotional states are likely to synch up more rapidly. For this reason, sitting in this posture can take you even deeper than simple eye-gazing, and you can sit Yab Yum as a time-out whenever you feel that conflict or disharmony are affecting your interactions.

With or without intercourse, if you sit in this position for a period of fifteen minutes or so (it may take a little practice to stay comfortable for this long), you are likely to become fully absorbed in one another. You may even feel that the outside world has slipped away and you are cocooned together in some other realm.

CHAPTER FORTY-SEVEN

Play with Polarities: Kali Asana

Kali Asana was probably the primary posture used in the earliest form of Tantric ceremony. You can see it in the Hindu Tantric art that shows various manifestations of the Goddess astride the supine and corpselike Shiva. The association of this posture with the Goddess Kali highlights its connection with the oldest aspects of the Tantric tradition. Kali is the supreme Goddess in Tantra. She is depicted as fierce and wrathful. She carries various weapons in her multiple arms. She wears a garland of skulls around her neck and a sash of human heads and arms around her waist. She holds a severed human head, which is said to represent the ego, in one of her hands.

Many Westerners associate this ferocious female deity either with something evil or with something filled with rage. We have heard more than one person refer to "letting Kali out," a euphemism for uncontrolled, angry venting. These interpretations can be supported by a very literal-minded look at the images, but they miss the esoteric meanings of all this ferocity, meanings that are considerably closer to the purpose of those early Tantric rituals. The symbolism of the severed head relates directly to questions of ego and attachment, and according to the oral tradition, if one surrenders to Kali and worships her, she transforms herself from wrathful deity to loving, nurturing mother. Perhaps even more to the point, it is said that Kali enables her devotees to triumph over fear. From this perspective, Kali can be seen as embodying and perhaps even surpassing those things in life that frighten us most. By facing the things we fear and making allies of them, we become more empowered as human beings, and what terrifies us most can become a source of strength.

This is only a superficial look at Kali and her iconography, but we thought it important to mention, both because there is so much misunderstanding and because of the connections between Kali Asana and the very origins of Tantra.

In the basic form of Kali Asana, Shiva lies prone and Shakti either sits or squats astride him. As with Yab Yum, this enables Shakti to control the pace from the moment of penetration, and Shakti is free to move; Shiva has somewhat more leverage for thrusting back and also has the option of remaining motionless. This allows for more variety than Yab Yum and is also usually more comfortable for both partners. Shakti not only sets the pace but can also have more control

Fig. 21: It is easy for Shiva to stroke Shakti's genitals in Kali Asana

over the depth of penetration. Shiva's hands are free, making it easier to stimulate Shakti's genitals manually, something that is considerably more difficult in Yab Yum.

In this position, a number of variations are possible. For Shakti: if you are sitting or squatting, it can be interesting to experiment with leaning forward or backward, since this changes the sensation in subtle but significant ways. It can also be very helpful to have a headboard or something similar that you can grab. For Shiva: try holding Shakti's buttocks for added support. This is a great position for becoming more skilled at regulating ejaculation. The key to developing this ability lies in learning to relax as you near the point of no return. If you are lying prone, it is much easier to let your entire body go limp. It can help to focus specifically on relaxing your thighs and/or your pelvic floor.

The variation on this position that is known as "reverse cowgirl" in American popular culture can produce intense sensations for both partners. If Shiva has male genitalia, the erect penis is being pressed in a direction that is the opposite of its normal orientation, and the frenulum receives more stimulation than in most other positions. Shakti's vagus nerve receives direct pressure from the head of the penis or dildo. While this is not a face-to face-position, it is a great one for watching yourselves in the mirror, a visual that many people find intensely erotic.

CHAPTER FORTY-EIGHT

An Old Standard Made New: Missionary with Enhancements

When we talk about Tantric sexual practices, we frequently encounter the misconception that Tantra is a form of sexual Yoga, with Yoga meaning physical gymnastics, and hence that Tantric sex is all about positions. Tantra and Yoga are, in fact, closely related, so much so that certain texts are claimed by both traditions, and the term *Tantric Yoga* is used by some practitioners. Just as physical postures are only one part of Yoga, sexual activity is only one part of Tantra, and as we have explained, the only truly Tantric sexual positions are Shakti-superior positions. Medieval Indian culture produced an impressive body of instructional erotic material, most notably the *Kama Sutra*, the *Koka Shastra*, and the *Ananga Ranga*. These texts are comprehensive sex manuals that describe an array of techniques and positions, but they are not part of the Tantric tradition.

You can approach any activity with a Tantric mindset, and that includes any sexual encounter. Your state of mind is what really matters. If you are thinking energetically, even the most familiar and seemingly mundane positions can be the source of new and unexpected pleasures. One way to make this a reality is to bring other erogenous zones into play during penetrative sex. This introduces additional points of contact, resulting in a more complex energetic exchange.

Most people think of the missionary position as somewhat staid, bland, and boring, as the name suggests. Of course, sex should never be staid, bland, and boring, even with the lights off and your eyes closed (something we don't recommend except as way of exploring sensory deprivation). The missionary position is part of our repertoire, and it's no less enjoyable for being conventional. If you want to make the missionary position even more interesting, you can experiment with a number of variations and observe how they change your experience.

The thumbs and big toes are erogenous zones with distinctly phallic overtones, and sucking them can be extremely erotic for both giver and receiver. In the missionary position it is easy for Shakti to suck Shiva's thumb. If you modify the position slightly, so that Shakti's legs are elevated, Shiva can suck Shakti's big toe. To complicate it in an even more delightful way, try doing each other simultaneously, so that Shiva sucks Shakti's toe while Shakti sucks Shiva's thumb.

The back of the knee is another erogenous zone that can be fairly readily accessible in the missionary position or a modified version thereof. The backs of the knees are a very sensitive and highly innervated

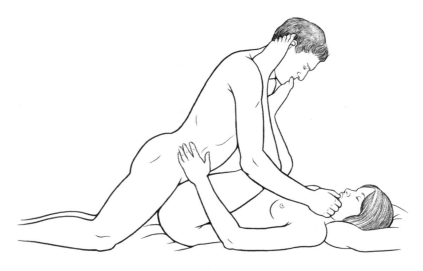

Fig. 22: When Shiva sucks Shakti's toe and Shakti sucks Shiva's thumb, an additional energetic circuit is created

part of the body, but they are not particularly sensitive as an erogenous zone until you are in a high state of arousal. Having them stroked when you are very turned on can be an interesting addition to missionary sex, if you can tune in to the subtle sensations this produces.

If you are embodying Shiva, press into Shakti's palms with yours; the palms too are erogenous zones that are responsive during high states of arousal. They are also recognized as centers that are particularly important for sending and receiving energy, as many healing practitioners are aware. Pressing the palms together can also be a form of holding down and restraining your partner. Hence, it is a gentle way of infusing your interactions with elements of power and surrender, dominance and submission. These elements are present in every sexual encounter, and one does not have to become a hardcore participant in the BDSM (bondage, discipline, dominance, submission, sadism, masochism) scene to recognize this aspect of sex and to play with it from time to time. Engaging with your eyes, as you hold your lover down, is a way to make this exchange even more intense, since the eyes transmit and receive energy, too.

CHAPTER FORTY-NINE

Doggy Style and Some New Tricks

Doggy style is another familiar and fairly conventional sexual position. Because it gives access to the back, it offers a number of interesting opportunities for stimulating additional erogenous zones and making energetic connections. Try some of these, and see how they work for you.

Stimulating the sacrum (the five fused vertebrae at the base of the spine, often called the small of the back) in this position can add to your partner's arousal. This area is very sensitive. The sacral nerves run from the sacrum to the genitals, as well as through the legs to the soles of the feet. These nerves play an important part in the orgasmic response, and stimulating them electrically has shown promise as a treatment for people who are unable to experience orgasm.[44]

The best way to engage the sacrum in this position is to tap gently at first with the fingertips of one hand. (You'll need the other to keep your balance and continue thrusting.) Next you can move into gentle percussion with the knife-edge of your hand, a soft karate chop. Check in to determine what feels best. You can also place the palm of your hand on the sacrum and rub, producing friction, or hold it in place and vibrate it. All of these methods can produce an intensified state of arousal.

Fig. 23: Pulling Shakti's hair from behind can build arousal

Shiva can also lean forward and blow upon, kiss, or bite the back of Shakti's neck. Many species of animal bite the back of the neck when mating. This is another important erogenous zone, and stimulating it impacts the parasympathetic nervous system. Think of baby mammals relaxing completely when picked up by the scruff of the neck. So try this if things are getting overheated, or if you simply want to invite your partner to surrender even more fully to the experience. You can also grab the hair at the nape of the neck and pull it gently.

If Shakti is being penetrated vaginally, Shiva can stimulate the anus at the same time, either externally or internally. While we don't generally recommend using the thumb for digital anal penetration, it is perfect for anal play in this position. Just applying the pressure of a well-lubricated thumb on the outside of the anus can be intensely pleasurable. You can go further and use it to penetrate, if that works for you both. As you know, the thumb is also an erogenous zone, so stimulating the anus with the thumb is yet another way of creating an additional energetic circuit while having penetrative sex.

Finally, Shakti can take a vibrator and stimulate Shiva's perineum. To do this, you will need to support yourself with one arm or shoulder as you reach around. It may be a bit of a challenge to keep the vibrator in place if you are highly aroused or if Shiva is thrusting vigorously. But it will be worth the effort. Chances are it will intensify the experience for both of you, especially if the vibrator is a strong one, since you will both feel the sensations. Save this one until Shiva is ready to have an orgasm because the stimulation can be very intense and is likely to push many people over the edge.

The possibilities for bringing additional erogenous zones into play during penetrative sex are virtually unlimited. We've given you a few basic suggestions. You can review the section on erotic trigger points, and explore stimulating them during intercourse in whatever position you like. Treat it as a creative venture; have fun, and be playful.

PART NINE

Expanding Orgasmic Response

While the evidence suggests that the earliest Tantric sex rituals were developed for the purpose of obtaining power through spirit possession—something that might not be considered "spiritual" by some—it is clear that by the seventh or eighth century CE, the focus had shifted. According to the *Vijnanabhairava Tantra*: "At the time of sexual intercourse with a woman, absorption into her is brought about by excitement, and the delight that ensues at orgasm betokens the delight of Brahman. This delight is in reality that of one's own self."[45]

A puritanical commentator, writing in the eighteenth century, suggested that this passage is intended symbolically and that the delight of orgasm is but a poor substitute for the "delight of Brahman." The commentator goes on to minimize the role of the partner, since the light resides within the self, and to assert that anyone who takes this text as advocating sexual pleasure is a fool. This type of commentary frequently accompanies references to sex in Tantric texts. Sometimes it is intended to obscure the explicitness of the message, and sometimes it is done in an effort to harmonize Tantric ideas with more conservative aspects of Hindu thought.

Whether or not the commentator on the *Vijnanabhairava* is correct, the passage points to something very significant. Thirteen centuries ago, Tantric practitioners understood that orgasm is a gateway to mystical states. As we understand the text, sex is one of many valid ways to reach these states.

According to the *Yoga Sutras* (the foundational Yogic text, attributed to Patanjali, and composed or compiled somewhere between the sixth and first centuries BCE), "Yoga is the cessation of the fluctuations of the mind-stuff," as Dr. Mumford translates it.[46] In orgasm, mental activity subsides, the ego may dissolve, and it's possible to feel a sense of merger, yoga, or union with one's beloved or even with the universe. This is how we understand the phrase "betokens the delight of Brahman." For this reason, Tantric practitioners, both ancient and modern, have developed a variety of methods for expanding, intensifying, and redefining orgasm, thus prolonging that mystical state so that it can last for more than a few seconds. Some of these are simple to learn; others take some practice; most are not very time-consuming, and all of them can transform your sexual life.

The popular belief that Tantric sex means extended lovemaking that goes on for hours and hours is inaccurate, but it isn't entirely wrong. Prolonging arousal is important, since it is one of the keys to transforming the fleeting mystical state we all can experience at the moment of orgasm into something that is more profound and enduring. The purpose is not stamina for its own sake. Prolonged sexual encounters can be delightful but not if you're watching the clock or damping down your arousal so that you can last. We've also discovered, through our own explorations, that it is possible to get to this mystical place even during somewhat shorter lovemaking sessions.

In a 1989 lecture, Dr. Mumford observed: "If you are talking about the sexual experience for a human being, you are talking about shifts in the human nervous system."[47] This observation was informed by his experience in traditional Tantra and his knowledge of Western science; however, Western science is just starting to catch up with what Tantric practitioners have understood for centuries, at least in general terms.

The development of advanced brain-imaging technology has made it possible to study the way the brain and nervous system function during sexual arousal and orgasm, although the data are incomplete and sometimes conflicting. At least one study suggests that there is decreased activity in the amygdala during penile stimulation.[48] This part of the brain plays an important role in triggering fear and anxiety, but it also reacts to appetitive stimuli. To complicate matters, other studies show amygdala activation at orgasm. Brain scans have also shown a deactivation of the left prefrontal cortex during a partner-stimulated clitoral orgasm. This part of the brain is "best known for its involvement in moral reasoning and social judgment," and the researchers suggested that the deactivation of this region "implies the absence of moral judgment and self-referential thought"—in other words, the cessation of the fluctuations (or at least many of the fluctuations) of the mindstuff.[49]

Just about everyone agrees that orgasms are pretty good. In Tantra, orgasms—and, perhaps more importantly, the whole process leading up to them—are recognized not just as good but also as being replete with transcendent potential. Although Tantric practice is not goal-oriented and we don't recommend focusing on "achieving" orgasms, they do open us up to mystical experiences, and our everyday orgasms are only the beginning. There are many ways to enrich and enhance orgasm and make it not only something that is felt in the body, but an experience that touches the mind and spirit as well. Once we abandon the idea that orgasm is something that only takes place in the genitals, we can have access to a whole new world of possibilities.

CHAPTER FIFTY

Simply Give and Receive

By now you probably understand that conscious exploration of polarities and the vast gray areas between them is a core aspect of the Tantric approach. In sex, this can mean bringing awareness to processes that are often ignored or taken for granted, which is an important part of the work. In Part Four, Kissing, we discussed giving and receiving kisses and described how sexual encounters frequently involve a kind of unspoken, unexamined process of exchange in which one person gives for a while, in hopes of receiving, and the other does the same. When this works well, and it can when people really tune in to each other, it can be highly arousing and spontaneous, but relying on chance and chemistry is not the best way to ensure that you're getting the most out of sex.

Armed with this understanding, Western teachers of sexual Neo-Tantra have come up with the concept of "Giving and Receiving Sessions." While this is not in any way a traditional practice, we see it as an innovation that is consistent with traditional principles. These sessions are valuable for developing sexual self-knowledge, knowledge of one's partner, and orgasmic skills. The basic concept is simple. One person gives the other a massage, culminating in one that focuses on the genitals. This is not done as foreplay, and the roles are clearly defined: one gives, and the other receives. When the massage is over, it is over, and the giver and receiver reverse roles on another day.

This approach to giving and receiving erotic pleasure removes the element of unspoken, unexamined exchange from the equation. It creates a circumstance in which the receiver simply receives and the giver simply gives. This affords you the opportunity to see just how deeply you can give and receive, without feeling the pressure of having to reciprocate and without intercourse, or even orgasm, as a goal. It also makes it possible for you to tell your partner what gives you pleasure and what doesn't work so well. It is crucial to provide this feedback in kind and supportive terms, since this exploration can be intense, and both giver and receiver are vulnerable.

We strongly encourage people to purchase a massage table. It's a relatively inexpensive item and one that is very useful for erotic exploration. Its uses are not limited to giving and receiving sessions, although it is particularly valuable in that context. If you don't have a massage table, you can do the session on a bed. You may want to bathe together before you begin. This can be a good time to discuss what, if anything, you'd like to focus on during the session. Be sure to create an environment that is warm and comfortable, and to add elements that evoke sensuality and eroticism. Begin the session with a full-body massage before moving into more directly erotic stimulation.

Giving and receiving sessions are a very good way to experiment sexually. If you have never received a prostate massage, this is a perfect context for seeing what it feels like. Remember that if it isn't particularly pleasant the first time, you may well develop an appreciation for it over several such sessions. The same is true for G-spot massage.

Giving and receiving sessions are also perhaps the easiest context for people with G-spots to learn how to have ejaculatory orgasms and for people with penises to learn how to have non-ejaculatory, full-body orgasms. Learning to ejaculate usually requires a willingness to bear down during the orgasm and also getting over the fear that you might urinate. In a giving and receiving session you can also express just how much pressure and intensity you want. Learning how to have a full-body, non-ejaculatory orgasm requires being stimulated and brought almost to the point of no return repeatedly, pulling back each time and using the imagination to direct the orgasmic energy back into the body (more on this in the next chapter).

For both types of orgasmic response, it takes practice. Remember you are opening up new neural pathways. You may also be redefining orgasm for yourself, since there is a widespread tendency to think of orgasm as a clitoral phenomenon experienced solely in the glans or as being synonymous with ejaculation. This process of redefinition is critical; recognizing that something is possible brings you much closer to being able to make it happen.

We want to reiterate that it is not clear whether everyone with female genitalia is capable of ejaculating, and some people may never enjoy receiving G-spot massage. Remember that human sexual response varies a great deal from person to person, and the purpose of exploration is to find and embrace whatever works for you. If, after a period of experimentation, you are not feeling pleasure or are feeling pleasure but not ejaculating, don't worry about it.

If you have male genitalia, it can be very useful to refrain from ejaculating during some receiving sessions, and it is important to do so, since it will help you learn to separate orgasm from ejaculation. Outside of this context, don't worry about what kind of orgasm you have. Some traditions, Taoism in particular, advocate non-ejaculation in varying degrees as a way of preserving the life force. We don't share this view, and there is now a body of research showing that frequent ejaculations are related to a reduced risk of prostate cancer. In one study, a group with a lifetime average of twenty-one ejaculations per month was 33.3 percent less likely to develop prostate cancer than those who averaged four to seven per month.[50]

Space precludes us from going into more detail about giving and receiving sessions, so we'd like to provide you with a few resources. If you are interested in specific genital massage strokes, we recommend Barbara Carrellas's *Urban Tantra* as a source.[51] If you are more visual, *Fire on the Mountain* and *Fire in the Valley* by Joseph Kramer and Annie Sprinkle are also great for instruction on specific strokes.[52] We discuss giving and receiving in more detail in *Tantra for Erotic Empowerment* and describe some wonderful massage techniques in

The Essence of Tantric Sexuality.[53] Our video *Tantric Sexual Massage for Lovers* depicts the use of these techniques as a precursor to genital massage.[54] These may all be useful if you wish to go a little deeper, but the information we've provided here should be more than enough to get you started.

CHAPTER FIFTY-ONE

Ride the Wave

Playing on the edge is more than just a tool for people who want to learn how to have full-body orgasms. For most of us, it is a delicious state in which to linger in its own right (a minority of people, particularly those who have difficulty climaxing, may feel frustrated by remaining on the edge for too long). In addition, remaining in this state for extended periods of time frequently intensifies the orgasmic experience, so much so that there is a fetish known as "edging" and a genre of pornographic material that focuses on the technique. Watching just one or two clips of skilled practitioners will illustrate just how intense edging can be.

People tend to think of orgasm in somewhat simplistic terms and to limit themselves to the scope of what is familiar to them. This is the biggest hurdle in learning how to have full-body orgasms, with or without erection. Once you understand that ejaculation and orgasm can be separated, it is much easier to make it a reality in your body. Similarly, it becomes much easier for people to become multiorgasmic or to think themselves off (generate an orgasm without physical stimulation), once they know that this is possible and begin developing the skill set. And the edge of orgasm is the place to do just that.

Exploring the edge can be done on your own or with a partner, and there is great value in both approaches. If prolonging arousal creates an altered state of consciousness, staying as close to the brink of orgasm for as long as you can is even more intense. Others have made an analogy between this process and surfing, and although we are not surfers, we suspect the analogy is an apt one. You have to be prepared to risk going over the edge. If you get overexcited, and your sympathetic nervous system kicks in, you will wipe out. If you back off too far, and your parasympathetic nervous system is overactive, your arousal will diminish or disappear. With some practice, you will develop the skill to remain within just the right zone, riding the crest of the wave. This will enable people with male genitalia to choose when and if to let go and have an ejaculatory orgasm.

People with female genitals generally have a broader range of orgasmic responses. Those who are multiorgasmic may not feel the need to play on the edge, since their arousal tends to drop only slightly after they come, if at all. If you are wired differently, playing on the edge may help you learn to have multiple orgasms. If doing this practice only leaves you frustrated, tottering on the brink but unfulfilled, then recognize that it doesn't work for you and move on, but don't do this hastily. Orgasms happen in the brain as well as in the body, and re-educating one or the other or both can take some time.

Playing on the edge during partnered sex can be especially delightful because you are both in this zone simultaneously. This kind of tandem surfing requires attunement and knowing your lover well, since it is very easy for the movements and excitement of one to send the other over the edge. Maintaining eye contact and awareness of breath are very helpful in this regard. Verbal communication is good, too, although many of us have difficulty expressing ourselves when we're very turned on. A simple "Stop," "Slow down," or a gesture will often do the trick. Withdrawal for brief periods is also an effective way to back off from the crest.

As you know, many people have the misconception that Tantric sex is all about extended lovemaking sessions. By now we should have disabused you of that idea. Prolonging and building arousal will induce an altered state of consciousness, provided a sufficiently high state of arousal is maintained. We generally recommend a minimum of half an hour for people who are just starting out. While prolonged lovemaking can be great, it is not always an option, especially for busy adults who have children and/or other obligations.

We have found that what we call a Tantric quickie can be a good substitute for longer sessions. It is perhaps not quite as intensely consciousness altering, but it is effective and very satisfying nonetheless. It only takes about ten minutes, although we don't recommend watching the clock. The technique involves building arousal very rapidly, bringing each other to that zone where it feels like you might reach the point of no return at any moment, and trying to remain in that zone until you both agree that it's time to let go. Multiorgasmic people may have a series of orgasms during this period. Just be sure that your arousal doesn't drop off and that you don't send your partner over the edge. This is a profoundly intimate and highly energized state to share. With a little practice you will learn to read each other and know when to let go, surrender, and let the waves crash around you.

CHAPTER FIFTY-TWO

Anal Sex
for Energy Activation

We have already written about the importance of the anus as an erogenous zone, the intensity of orgasms that are experienced in conjunction with prostate massage, and some of the ways in which anal penetration can provide those with male genitalia with something that approximates being vaginally penetrated. Nonetheless, there is more to say on the subject, both from the perspective of contemporary scientific understandings and from a more traditionally Tantric standpoint.

You have already read about some basic concepts pertaining to energy, prana, and the chakra system. These are complex and often esoteric subjects, and others have written entire books on them. Nevertheless, we'd like to expose you to an additional term that may be familiar to some: *Kundalini*. If you do an Internet search for the word, your results will likely include explanations that may seem baffling or perhaps even frightening. Like Tantra, Kundalini is a term that has produced a voluminous body of literature, much of it mystifying. At the most basic level, there is no need to be afraid of this energy, and it can be explained in fairly simple terms.

In the classical literature, this energy is described as dwelling at the base of the spine in the form of a coiled serpent. When awakened, the energy is said to move up the spine, piercing the chakras and leading to profound and sometimes permanent changes in consciousness. Some of the modern literature on the subject has suggested that this is an enlightened state that is sometimes mistaken for (and can be hard to distinguish from) mental illness.[55] The experience of a "Kundalini awakening" is sought by some and feared by others. In our lineage, the understanding is that Kundalini is present and active in all of us, that it is essentially our personal concentrated dose of prana, and that its activity increases during sexual arousal, among other states. From this perspective, there is nothing to fear from Kundalini, since it is the life force that exists within us at all times. The key is to become conscious of and able to tap into this energy when you choose to do so.

Like other forms of energy, Kundalini is given feminine attributes and is worshipped as a goddess. This is very interesting in the context of the complexities of gender that we have discussed; snakes generally have phallic associations, and the movement of Kundalini is portrayed as a form of penetration. Thus, in some respects, Kundalini itself can be understood as representing the inner fusion of the masculine and feminine aspects we all contain.

So Kundalini is imagined as being a coiled serpent, dwelling at the base of the spine, in the first chakra. It is even said that there is a gland at the base of the spine in which the energy resides. As you already know, there are various Tantric and Yogic practices that involve anal or pubococcygeal muscle contractions or locks. In the broadest possible terms, one of the main purposes of doing these contractions is to activate the Kundalini energy. Another way to understand the function of the pulses is to think of them as either bringing our awareness to, or increasing the movement of, energy that is always active within us. The Kriya Yoga practices into which we've been initiated begin with pranayamas and anal/pubococcygeal contractions for this reason. Some contend that anal sex is one of the most direct and effective ways to activate the flow of Kundalini.

There is great value in, and much pleasure to be enjoyed from, anal intercourse, whether or not you believe in Kundalini energy. Because we associate the anus with excretion and are likely to think of it as unclean, we tend to forget that it is actually part of our sexual apparatus. For some people receiving anal intercourse produces the most deeply satisfying orgasms. Regardless of how we may feel about it, the pubococcygeal muscles stretch from front to back, connecting the anus and the genitals. Although experienced Tantric practitioners can isolate segments of the PC muscles and pulse where they choose, there's something they can't control—the reflexive pulsing of the anus at orgasm.

Depending on your relationship configuration, the use of strap-on dildos will make it possible for both partners to experience anal intercourse. As with oral sex, there are strong cultural tendencies to view receiving anal sex as both degrading and submissive, or as a sign of being homosexual. Of course none of this is true biologically; we can enjoy anal sex simply because we all have an abundance of nerve endings in this part of the body. Nevertheless, beliefs and taboos are hard to eradicate. The Tantric approach to living invites us to transcend limiting beliefs and discover for ourselves. If nothing pleasurable happens after a series of sessions, you can decide that the activity is not for you, and that's fine. You will have discovered something for yourself.

Safer-sex practices are of course important when having anal sex and are generally a good idea even if you are fluid-bonded or are using a strap-on. It is also helpful to be as clean as possible before attempting anal intercourse. Perfect cleanliness is inhuman, so getting over any squeamishness you may have is recommended as well. Be sure you have generous quantities of lube on hand, and if you are using latex condoms, be sure that the lube is water or silicone based. Never use Vaseline or any petroleum-based product, and don't use silicone lube with silicone toys. There are many high-quality lubricants on the market today, some specifically intended for anal sex.

There are some important practical considerations to bear in mind. Remember to go slowly and to do a lot of warm-up. This may include external massage; analingus—stimulating the anus with the mouth and tongue (if you feel uncomfortable about doing this or are not fluid-bonded, be sure to use a dental dam, plastic wrap, or other impermeable barrier for making oral-genital or oral-anal contact safer); the insertion of sex toys to relax the muscles; and penetration with a finger. As with digital stimulation, the experience is far more likely to be pleasurable if the person receiving is in a high state of arousal before being entered, and thrusting too rapidly or with too much force is not likely to be pleasant, especially for the inexperienced. As is true with virtually every form of sex, finding the right balance between relaxation and arousal is the key to making it enjoyable.

There is no one position in which it is easiest to receive, and responses vary from person to person. A modified version of the missionary position is best for some people. Lying face down can also work well, but it requires a lot of awareness on the part of the penetrator, since it allows for very deep entry and limits the receiver's ability to move. Others prefer doggy style, and as we have already discussed, receiver-superior positions such as reverse cowgirl allow the person being penetrated to set the pace and control the depth. If you are interested in learning more about the ins and outs of anal sex, we highly recommend Tristan Taormino's *The Ultimate Guide to Anal Sex for Women* (regardless of your gender) and *The Anal Sex Position Guide,* as well as Jack Morin's *Anal Pleasure and Health: A Guide for Men, Women and Couples.*[56] These books will give you detailed information that can supplement your experiential knowledge. As always, we encourage you to experiment and enjoy.

CHAPTER FIFTY-THREE

Break Your Patterns
to Discover New Sensations

By now you should have a very clear sense that expanding the range of one's sexual response, both mentally and physiologically, is an important aspect of the Tantric approach. We have discussed the value of engaging additional erogenous zones in conjunction with genital stimulation, both as a way of creating energetic circuits and as a way of developing a richer erotic palette. If you add stimulation and/or change the manner of stimulation at the point of climax, you may find that you have new orgasmic experiences that are different from the familiar ones.

The conventional model of heterosexual sex involves "foreplay," which may include kissing, stimulation of the erogenous zones, and manual or oral genital contact, all leading up to genital intercourse. Even if this is not your personal model, people in general tend to narrow their focus as orgasm approaches and will often keep doing the same thing, perhaps a little more vigorously, to bring themselves or their partners to orgasm. There is nothing wrong with having sex this way. It can be very enjoyable, but interesting things can happen if you break the pattern and try something different.

This is an advanced technique, and it may not be for everyone, especially people who are, as Nina Hartley refers to them, "hard comes."[57] That is to say, they require a lot of stimulation and may need everything to be just right in order to experience orgasm. Even if you are not a hard come, this technique may not always work for you, since it can short-circuit the orgasmic response. It is probably best to begin exploring this through self-pleasuring, but it can be very interesting in the context of partnered sex as well, provided you have a solid relationship founded on trust, share an experimental attitude, and recognize that experiments are not always successful. Know that if you are not thrilled with the outcome, it is nobody's fault.

Changing the rate, intensity, or manner of genital stimulation can be distracting for some, resulting in a drop of arousal and perhaps in frustration, but again, if you are in a trusting relationship that embraces experimentation, give it a try. For example, during penetrative intercourse, go completely still and relax all your muscles as the sensation of orgasmic inevitability hits you. If you are performing cunnilingus, shift from licking to sucking on the clitoris at the last possible moment (this may require the receiver to alert you). If you are performing fellatio, switch from oral stimulation to manual when you feel your partner is about to ejaculate. While many people have the idea that the ideal blowjob involves swallowing, this change in stimulation can result in a very intense orgasm, especially if you have kept your partner on the brink for a while. There are numerous possibilities for changing the pattern and pace of stimulation, and if you don't find it frustrating, it is a great way to add variety and new sensations to your sex life.

Whether or not changing stimulation in the way we've just described is something you enjoy, the easiest approach is to add something new. We have alluded to this previously in the context of self-pleasuring and in creating energetic circuits using erotic trigger points. When you bring this into play as your partner reaches the point of no return, it can serve to intensify orgasm, and sometimes taking a person by surprise in this context can be an added enhancement. The mind can get somewhat boggled, and this creates an opening for discovering new sensations, moving us beyond our preconceptions about what we like and what we don't.

You can use some of the points we have already described, and just bring them in at the very apex. Sucking on something at this moment—for instance, your lover's fingers—can be very effective, since oral pleasures are so primal. Playing with the nipples also works well, as does slapping the buttocks. Of course, people do this kind of thing in the context of regular lovemaking (and multiplying the stimulation is one of the reasons that many people enjoy group sex), but we're talking about something very specific here—waiting until the last possible moment to add the secondary contact.

These practices may be particularly helpful for those who have difficulty experiencing orgasm as anything more than a genital phenomenon. Engaging other parts of the body, just as you are approaching the peak, creates a whole new series of sensations that you will begin to associate with orgasm. If you can visualize or imagine that the orgasm is happening not only in your genitals but also in the other area being stimulated, you may eventually be able to feel it there as well.

CHAPTER FIFTY-FOUR

Breathing as an Alchemical Practice

By now you should have a fairly good understanding of the role of breath in the Tantric tradition and some experiential knowledge of how to work with your breath. You've observed and changed your pattern of breathing at orgasm while self-pleasuring. You've learned to use breathing together as a tool for creating harmony. You've also learned about reciprocal breathing in the context of kissing, including during intercourse. Although it is a great way to build intimacy and amp up arousal, the kind of reciprocal breathing we described in chapter 22 is very difficult, if not impossible, to sustain just before and during orgasm. It demands too much focus and coordination, and keeping your mouths locked together as one or both of you comes is physically restricting and can result in chipped teeth or bitten lips or tongues. Nevertheless, there are some very interesting things you can do with the breath in these heightened states of arousal, building on the knowledge you already have.

When you're approaching, moving into and through orgasm, you can use breathing as a form of communication and energetic exchange. It is one of the easiest ways to take each other higher and higher. While most yogic breathing is done through the nose, it is much easier to do partnered breathing through the mouth, especially when you are very excited. Doing so adds the element of sound to the process but also makes it much easier to stay in synch. If you are facing each other, you can gaze into each other's eyes as you breathe. This will intensify the energetic exchange.

Breathing simultaneously is generally the easiest approach, and when accompanied by sound and eye-gazing, it is likely to produce very strong orgasms. Breathing reciprocally (but not exchanging breath), one of you inhaling as the other exhales and vice versa, requires more coordination, especially when you're very turned on. Doing so will probably change the experience; instead of pumping up the energy together, you are thrusting it back and forth. This creates a kind of ebb and flow that many find pleasurable. You may also find it interesting to explore how the feeling of breathing in opposition differs depending on whether you are being penetrated or are doing the penetrating.

You can try a number of variations, as you did when you changed your breathing pattern at orgasm. These include shallow breaths, breathing from the middle of your lungs, and breathing deeply. Different paces are also likely to alter the experience for you both, with panting having one effect, and slow deep breaths another.

We'd like to conclude this last tip by introducing you to a very simplified form of a practice that comes out of *Kriya Yoga*, a tradition that is closely related to Tantra. Kriya means "action," and kriyas generally involve breath, subtle movements, and often the mental repetition of a mantra. This can be a very effective way of working with sexual energy in the body. Although most Kriya Yoga lineages are ascetic and do not suggest that kriyas should be employed in the context of sexual activity, their use in conjunction with sex can be quite profound.

Certain advanced Tantric practitioners actually have the ability to perform a type of vajroli mudra that involves drawing fluids into the body through the urethra. In some of the ancient rituals we described, instead of exchanging fluids by consuming them, these adepts would ejaculate and then draw the commingled sexual fluids back into their bodies using this technique. As we see it, there is no need to master this physical practice, since visualizing it works very well. In addition, by using the imagination in conjunction with this simplified kriya, anatomy is not an issue, and people of all genders can imagine that they are drawing the combined sexual energy up the spine and into the skull and then allowing it to flow back down again. This practice builds intimacy and often produces very intense sensations.

Performing the kriya involves a few simple steps. First, tighten your pubococcygeal muscles. For those who have developed the ability to isolate them, focus on the anus. Inhale and imagine that you are pulling the energy up from your pelvic floor (either up your spine or through an imaginary tube in the middle of your body) until it reaches your skull. Once your lungs are almost full, take a sniff of air and tuck your chin. Hold your breath for as long as is comfortable. Exhale slowly and imagine that the energy is flowing back down your body, bathing you in warmth and re-concentrating in your pelvic bowl.

You can try this technique at any point during your lovemaking. If you choose to do it after orgasm, you can visualize that the energy you are drawing up is actually your commingled sexual fluids. You can do this whether you've actually exchanged these essences or not. It can be very effective to imagine that the union of your secretions has been

Fig. 24: Movement of energy in a basic sexual kriya

Fig. 25: Circulation of energy in an accelerated sexual kriya

transformed into radiant golden light and to draw this up the spine. Try doing three repetitions of this kriya.

Once you've become skilled at the simpler version, you can intensify the exchange by bringing your foreheads together in what is sometimes called a *third-eye kiss*. For this variation, you should imagine that the energy is circulating between you in a continuous loop, from the genitals, out the forehead (third eye), through your partner, and back again.

By doing either form of this kriya, you are creating a powerful mental image of a sharing that is far deeper than what most people experience in conventional intercourse. Each of you is entering the other, and you are suffusing each other's bodies with your combined essences. As with so many Tantric practices, what you believe is not particularly relevant. Your imagination is the key. Imagine this communion and keep on imagining it. It will become real for you.

Afterword

We've reached the end of this particular Tantric journey. We hope you've enjoyed your exploration and gained some new insights into yourself and your sexuality. We also hope you have more insight into the Tantric tradition and the role of sex in Tantra. It is our mission to bring more pleasure and happiness into people's lives, and if even one or two of the tips in *Great Sex Made Simple* had that effect on you, then we have succeeded.

Our initial vision was to create an accessible book that demystified Tantric sex and provided practical techniques that were easy for anyone to understand and employ. As we were writing, we found ourselves adding more advanced and complex material that was not exclusively aimed at the beginner. Rather than back off from this more advanced approach and dumb the material down, we chose to respect our readers. We decided to trust that this more advanced material could be presented in plain language and that even those with no prior experience could put these techniques into practice and benefit from doing so. If reading our book was your first exposure to Tantra, it's to your credit that you've stayed with it all the way to the end. It's said that Tantra is the way of the hero, and part of being heroic is being willing to stretch yourself—to push your limits, to be open to new ideas, to explore, and to think for yourself. So, congratulations!

This book also represents a kind of culmination for us. It is the third book in a trilogy dealing with Tantric sexuality (although there is certainly more to be said about the subject). We started writing our first book on Tantra, *The Essence of Tantric Sexuality*, back in 2005. In addition to being based on the seminal lectures Dr. Mumford presented at Llewellyn's Gnosticon Festival in the 1970s, *Essence* is an in-depth examination of Tantric theory and practice. It also includes a good many nonsexual techniques. It is at once a tribute and an attempt to make sure our Guru's teachings on sexual Tantra receive the recognition they so richly deserve.

Our second book, *Tantra for Erotic Empowerment*, is a workbook, designed to give people an experiential understanding of Tantra by using sexual exploration as an entry point. It focuses heavily on doing exercises, journaling, and observing oneself as the keys to developing a Tantric attitude. It is a detailed expression of our perspective on what it means to live a Tantric life, both in and out of the bedroom.

When we started writing *Essence*, we did not have a trilogy in mind, and the concept did not reveal itself to us until we completed our first draft of *Great Sex Made Simple*. We now have a clearer sense of how the three books are interrelated, representing a fairly comprehensive exposition of our understanding of Tantric sex from three somewhat different angles. If you are new to Tantra, and our book has inspired you to learn more about this subject, we suggest you continue with *Tantra for Erotic Empowerment* and then move on to *The Essence of Tantric Sexuality*, which is considerably more esoteric in focus.

For a somewhat different point of view and approach, we recommend our dear friend Barbara Carrellas's *Urban Tantra*. We're very grateful to Barbara for writing the foreword to this book. She is an incredible teacher and a person of great integrity, someone whose work we can endorse wholeheartedly. It has been our privilege to co-present with her on a number of occasions.

If you're interested in learning more about the Tantric tradition and want to receive authentic teachings and experiential knowledge of the vast array of nonsexual practices, something that will also enhance and enrich your experience of sex, it is still possible to study personally with Dr. Mumford online (www.jonnmumfordconsult

.com). His courses (which we have been administering since 2001) require self-discipline, but they are immensely rewarding for those who are willing to make the effort. Studying online with a teacher of Dr. Mumford's stature and commitment to his students is more intimate than attending a series of weekend workshops. Because the work is done on an ongoing basis, and the communication is regular, there's an opportunity to go very deep. This approach is not for everyone, but for those who are suited to it, the experience can be extraordinary.

Of course, you may not feel the need to do any further study at all, and that's fine. We've offered a variety of techniques in the preceding pages, enough to last most people many years if not a lifetime. There's something to be said for ending the search for new and better techniques and more information, for stopping where you are and just being. Whatever you do, we hope you never forget to find the pleasure in this moment, and the next, and the next . . .

Acknowledgments

We are indebted to our teacher, Dr. Jonn Mumford (Swami Anandakapila Saraswati), and several others with whom we have studied: Bhagavan Das, Dr. Rudolph Ballentine, and Daniel Odier. Each of them has had a profound influence on us, and on our thinking, writing, and teaching. Our relationship with Dr. Mumford has been an ongoing source of inspiration for more than a decade, and all three of our books have drawn on that source.

The original concept and proposal for *Great Sex Made Simple* took shape in a Media Bistro workshop led by Ryan Harbage. Ryan is a fantastic teacher, and we are very grateful to have had his guidance. We're also grateful to our fellow students in the workshop. Media Bistro (www.mediabistro.com) offers an array of classes and is a great resource for writers, whether novice or veteran.

It has been our privilege to collaborate with Barbara Carrellas (www.barbaracarrellas.com) on a number of projects, and we were thrilled when she agreed to write the foreword. Barbara also gave us much-needed support and encouragement at a crucial moment.

Damon Ginandes, Marc Clark, Jen Goldman, and Nan Wise (PhD candidate, Cognitive Neuroscience, Rutgers University) all provided invaluable feedback on the manuscript at various points. We appreciate their insights and have incorporated many of their suggestions. Nan stepped in on very short notice to ensure the accuracy of the scientific content.

Thanks to Adrian Buckmaster (www.adrianbuckmaster.com) for his wonderful photographs and his friendship over the years. Adrian is not only an outstanding photographer, he's also an astute editor and was the first person to read and comment on our earliest draft. Thanks also to Irene Delgado for her help during the photo session.

We're grateful to our agent, Malaga Baldi, for her hard work and tenacity; to Carrie Obry, formerly our editor at Llewellyn World-wide, for her belief in us; to Angela Wix, our current editor, for all her efforts on our behalf; and to the rest of the staff at Llewellyn for making *Great Sex Made Simple* a reality.

We're thankful to Rev. Jenellen Fischer (www.spankingforwellness.com) for helping to give us a final push in birthing this book.

Finally, we consider ourselves very fortunate to be part of the growing, global sex-positive community. Our friends, colleagues, and acquaintances from the Pleasure Salon (www.pleasuresalon.com) and elsewhere are a source of inspiration and strength. The Buddha once defined the spiritual life as "good fellowship," and in an increasingly atomized world, it is a privilege to share the journey with such an interesting and diverse group of fellow travelers.

Notes

INTRODUCTION

1. Mark A. Michaels and Patricia Johnson, *The Essence of Tantric Sexuality* (Woodbury, MN: Llewellyn Worldwide, 2007), pp. 1–2. "Tool for expansion" is one of several definitions Dr. Mumford uses. It does not appear in such succinct form in his published work, but he has frequently expressed it just this way in personal communications and in conversation.

PART 1: THE FUNDAMENTALS: KEY CONCEPTS AND ATTITUDES

2. Hugh B. Urban, *Tantra: Sex, Secrecy, and Power in the Study of Religion* (Berkeley: University of California Press, 2003). Urban provides a good overview of the role of secrecy in Tantra.

3. Mark A. Michaels and Patricia Johnson, *Secrets of Sacred Sex: The Essence of Tantric Sexuality* (Delhi, India: Moltilal Banarsidass, 2011). The Alexander Institute, *Advanced Tantric Sex Secrets* DVD, 2008.

CHAPTER 4. TAKE YOUR TIME

4. Diana Richardson, *Slow Sex: The Path to Fulfilling and Sustainable Sexuality* (Rochester, VT: Destiny Books, 2011); Nicole Daedone, *Slow Sex: The Art and Craft of Female Orgasm* (New York: Grand Central Publishing, 2011); and Belisa Vranich, "Why Slow Sex is Better: Like a Bottle of Fine Wine, Great Sex Takes Time," *Men's Fitness*, http://www.mensfitness.com/women/sex-tips/why-slow-sex-is-better. Accessed September 26, 2012.

CHAPTER 5. BUILD EXCITEMENT
AND PROLONG AROUSAL

5. John Horgan, "The God Experiments," *Discover Magazine*, December 2006. http://discovermagazine.com/2006/dec/god-experiments /article_view?b_start:int=1&-C. Accessed September 5, 2011. The article discusses the similarities between mystical experience and orgasm in the brain. A more recent study suggests that while there are many subjective similarities between the orgasmic and meditative experiences, the brain areas involved are different; however, the study seems to have focused on a limited number of meditative approaches and does not seem to have considered how combining meditation with sex might affect the brain, or how extending arousal might affect brain function. Nadia Webb, "The Neurobiology of Bliss—Sacred and Profane: Sex in the Brain and What It Reveals about the Neuroscience of Deep Pleasure," *Scientific American*, July 12, 2011. Online at http:// www.scientificamerican.com/article.cfm?id=the-neurobiology-of -bliss-sacred-and-profane. Accessed September 5, 2011.

CHAPTER 6: BE PRESENT

6. David Eagleman, "10 Unsolved Mysteries of the Brain: What We Know—and Don't Know—About How We Think," *Discover Magazine*, August 2007. http://discovermagazine.com/2007/aug/unsolved -brain-mysteries/article_view?b_start:int=0&-C. Accessed September 5, 2011. As Eagleman's article explains, not only are experiences in the past when we process them, our senses register events at different rates, and our brains then synchronize the divergent sense impressions.

PART 2: SELF-PLEASURING

7. "Oprah Talks Masturbation," *The Huffington Post*, January 17, 2008. http://www.huffingtonpost.com/2008/01/17/oprah-talks -masturbation_n_82070.html. Accessed September 5, 2011. See also, Joan Z. Shore, "Politically Correct Sex (for Women)," *The Huffington Post,* January 22, 2008. http://www.huffingtonpost.com/joan-z-shore /politically-correct-sex-f_b_82689.html. Accessed September 5, 2011. Shore's is a sharply critical take on "self-cultivation."

CHAPTER 10. PLEASURE YOURSELF
IN FRONT OF YOUR PARTNER

8. Patchen Barrs, *The Erotic Engine: How Pornography Has Powered Mass Communication, from Gutenberg to Google* (Toronto: Anchor Canada, 2010).

CHAPTER 11. USE A VIBRATOR:
IT'S MORE THAN JUST A SEX TOY

9. Hillary Howard, "Vibrators Carry the Conversation," *New York Times*, April 21, 2011, E1. http://www.nytimes.com/2011/04/21 /fashion/21VIBRATORS.html?pagewanted=all. Accessed September 5, 2011.

10. Rachel P. Maines, *The Technology of Orgasm: "Hysteria," the Vibrator, and Women's Sexual Satisfaction* (Baltimore, MD: Johns Hopkins University Press, 2001). Maines's book is an engaging and comprehensive history of the vibrator.

CHAPTER 12. FANTASIZE FREELY

11. Nancy Friday, *My Secret Garden: Women's Sexual Fantasies* (New York: Trident, 1973). Friday went on to write a number of other books in the same vein. *My Secret Garden* remains in print nearly forty years after it was first published.

12. Bill Herring, "What Is Sexual Sobriety?" July 10, 2009, billherring .info/atlanta_counseling/definition-of-sexual-sobriety. Accessed September 5, 2011. Herring describes sexual fantasy as a "boundary," which he claims is "like a warning track on a baseball outfield, signaling an imminent collision without a change of course."

13. Patrick Carnes, "The Ten Types #1—Fantasy Sex," http://www .iitap.com/documents/SDI-R%20The%20Ten%20Types%20-%20 Long%20Version.pdf. Accessed September 5, 2011. Patrick Carnes, *Don't Call It Love: Recovery from Sexual Addiction* (New York: Bantam, 1992), 285–86.

14. Dr. Dale A. Robbins, "About Sex and Marriage," http://www.victorious .org/sex.htm. Accessed September 5, 2011. Robbins's perspective is but one example of the prevailing conservative Christian attitude toward fantasy.

15. Kerry Sheldon and Dennis Howitt, "Sexual fantasy in paedophile offenders: Can any model explain satisfactorily new findings from a

study of Internet and contact sexual offenders?" *Legal and Criminological Psychology*, Volume 13, Issue 1, pp. 137–58, February 2008.

16. Brett Kahr, *Sex and the Psyche* (London: Penguin, 2007), excerpted as "Sexual Fantasies: All in the Mind" in *The Times* (London), online edition, February 7, 2007, http://women.timesonline .co.uk/tol/life_and_style/women/relationships/article1341377 .ece?token=null&offset=0&page=1. Accessed September 5, 2011.

PART 3: BEYOND WORDS:
SILENT WAYS TO CREATE INTIMACY
AND REVERENCE
CHAPTER 14. GAZE INTO EACH OTHER'S EYES

17. H. A. Sackheim, R. C. Gur, and M. C. Saucy, "Emotions Are Expressed More Intensely on the Left Side of the Face," *Science*, October 27, 1978, 202 (4366): 434–36. Abstract: http://www.sciencemag.org /content/202/4366/434.abstract. Accessed September 5, 2011.

CHAPTER 15. KEEP IN TOUCH

18. Dr. Jonn Mumford in Michaels and Johnson, *The Essence of Tantric Sexuality*, p. 31.

CHAPTER 18. BOW TO EACH OTHER

19. Media Matters for America, "Conservative Media Continue Tired Obsession with Obama's Supposed 'Bowing,'" April 13, 2010. http:// mediamatters.org/research/201004130016. Accessed September 5, 2011.

20. Bhagavan Das compared bowing to ducking in a class we attended more than a decade ago. The statement has stayed with us.

PART 4: KISSING
CHAPTER 23. PLAY WITH CUPID'S BOW

21. Karen Hart, "Face Reader; Rose Rosetree, 58, Sterling," *The Washington Post*, June 18, 2006, M3. http://pqasb.pqarchiver.com/washington post/access/1062128911.html?FMT=ABS&FMTS=ABS:FT&date= Jun+18%2C+2006&author=Karen+Hart&desc=Face+Reader%3B+ Rose+Rosetree%2C+58%2C+Sterling. Accessed September 5, 2011. Full article at http://www.rose-rosetree.com/SundaySource.htm. Accessed September 5, 2011. See also "How to Tell If You Have a High Sex Drive," http://answers.yahoo.com/question/index?qid=20080403

161048AAIpgM8. Accessed September 5, 2011. These items describe some of the beliefs about the philtrum and sex drive that exist in both Western and Asian traditions.

22. Stuart Brody and Rui Miguel Costa, "Vaginal Orgasm Is More Prevalent in Women with a Prominent Tubercle of the Upper Lip," *The Journal of Sexual Medicine*, June 15, 2001. Abstract: http:// onlinelibrary.wiley.com/doi/10.1111/j.1743-6109.2011.02331.x /abstract. Accessed September 5, 2011.

23. Henry C. Lu, *Traditional Chinese Medicine: How to Maintain Your Health and Treat Illness* (Laguna Beach, CA: Basic Health Publications, 2005), p. 89. Lu describes the role of the philtrum in acupuncture.

CHAPTER 24. EXCHANGE ESSENCES

24. David Gordon White, *Kiss of the Yogini: "Tantric Sex" in Its South Asian Contexts* (Chicago: University of Chicago Press, 2006).

25. Christiane Northrup, *Women's Bodies, Women's Wisdom: Creating Physical and Emotional Health and Healing*, revised edition (New York: Random House, 2010), pp. 233–34. Northrup's writing on "amrita" reveals how this conflation has reached the mainstream.

PART 5: AWAKENING THE SENSES
CHAPTER 25. SMELL

26. Dr. Kevin Kelliher, http://www.sci.uidaho.edu/biosci/labs/kelliher /research.htm. Accessed September 5, 2011. Scientific understanding of the sense of smell is evolving, and the bright-line distinction between the roles of the main and accessory olfactory systems is no longer accepted.

27. Johan N. Lundström, Julie A. Boyle, Robert J. Zatorre, and Marilyn Jones-Gotman, "The Neuronal Substrates of Human Olfactory Based Kin Recognition," *Human Brain Mapping* 30:8, 2571–80, August 2009.

CHAPTER 26. TASTE

28. Molly Birnbaum, *Season to Taste: How I Lost My Sense of Smell and Found My Way* (New York: HarperCollins, 2011). Birnbaum's memoir is a personal account that illuminates the intimate connection between smell and taste. For wine tasting, see Jonah Lerner, "The Subjectivity of Wine," *Scienceblogs*, November 2, 2007. http://scienceblogs.com/

cortex/2007/11/the_subjectivity_of_wine.php. Accessed September 5, 2011. Lerner describes several such experiments with wine drinkers.

29. We're grateful to our friend Jonathan Pratt, owner of Umami Café (www.umamicafe.com), for explaining the five tastes to us.

30. http://www.umamiinfo.com/2011/02/the-discovery-of-umami.php. Accessed September 5, 2011. Although umami has been recognized as a taste for more than a millennium in Japan, it was only scientifically accepted as such in the 1980s.

CHAPTER 27. SIGHT

31. Richard Restak, *The Secret Life of the Brain* (Washington, DC: Joseph Henry Press, 2001) pp. 19–31. Restak provides a good, brief overview of how sight develops in the first year of life and issues that may arise.

32. Turhan Conlee and John D. E. Gabrieli, "Imaging Gender Differences in Sexual Arousal," *Nature Neuroscience* 7:4, 325–26 (2004). http://homepage.psy.utexas.edu/Homepage/Group/MestonLAB /Publications/brain.pdf. Accessed September 5, 2011. There is much conflicting data on gender and responses to erotica, including with regard to brain function. This is a highly contested area, and the authors of this study that found significant gender differences in reactions to softcore and hardcore material (despite self-reporting to the contrary) pointed to another study that reached the opposite conclusion—that while men reported greater arousal, there were no detectable differences in brain function. The authors also make it clear that the recruitment process for studies of this type calls the results into question.

CHAPTER 28. TOUCH

33. Michaels and Johnson, *The Essence of Tantric Sexuality*, p. 96.

CHAPTER 29. HEARING

34. Jaideva Singh, trans., *The Yoga of Delight, Wonder, and Astonishment: A Translation of the Vijnana-bhairava* (Albany: State University of New York Press, 1991), p. 39.

PART 6: EROTIC TRIGGER POINTS
CHAPTER 31. NAPE OF THE NECK

35. "What Does a Kiss on the Neck Mean," FreeDating411.com, http:// www.freedating411.com/kissing/What-Does-A-Kiss-On-The-Neck

-Mean.html. Accessed September 5, 2011. The site also ascribes meaning to kisses on other parts of the body, claiming that a kiss on the lips conveys a message of attraction, not desire.

CHAPTER 40. G-SPOT

36. "The vulva contains a tube shaped to the penis, which is the swing in which the Love-God resides. Opened with two fingers, it causes the love-juice to flow . . . not far from it (the clitoris) within the vulva is a duct purnachandra (full moon), which is filled with this juice . . ." Alex Comfort, trans., *The Koka Shastra and Other Medieval Indian Writings on Love* (New York: Stein and Day, 1965), 154. This passage seems to provide instructions on digital stimulation of the G-spot, as a precursor to intercourse. Comfort suggests that the duct is the Bartholin's duct, but the passage does not evoke lubrication; the location described is not consistent with the location of the Bartholin's ducts, and the reference to the full moon is suggestive of the larger quantity of fluid associated with ejaculation.

PART 7: ENHANCING ORAL SEX

37. Annie Auguste, "The History of Fellatio," *Salon*, May 22, 2000. http:// www.salon.com/sex/feature/2000/05/22/oral_history/print.html. Accessed September 5, 2011. The survey is mentioned in this online interview with Thierry Leguay, a French author, whose book *Histoire raisonnée de la fellation* (History of Fellatio) has not been translated into English. The article also includes some interesting bits of information on attitudes toward fellatio in different cultures.

38. Adena N. Galinsky and Freya L. Sonenstein, "The Association of Developmental Assets and Sexual Enjoyment Among Emerging Adults," *Journal of Adolescent Health* 48:6, 610–15 (June 2011). The study also found that, in men, self-esteem was linked to the enjoyment of giving oral sex.

39. "Question: Is the Usage of Toys Allowed During Sexual Intercourse?" *Catholic Writings*, http://catholicwriter.wordpress.com/2006/09/13 /question-is-the-usage-of-sex-toys-allowed-during-sexual -intercourse/. Accessed September 5, 2011.

40. Fr. Stephen F. Torraco, "Is It a Sin for a Married Couple to Have Oral Sex with Each Other?" EWTN, Global Catholic Network, http://www .ewtn.com/vexperts/showmessage.asp?number=507442&Pg=Forum5 &Pgnu=1&recnu. Accessed September 5, 2011.

41. Michaels and Johnson, *The Essence of Tantric Sexuality*, p. 116.

PART 8: SEX POSITIONS: A TANTRIC TWIST

42. White, *Kiss of the Yogini*, pp. 8–13. We think White's arguments about the origins and early history of Tantra are compelling.

43. Dr. Jonn Mumford, *Ecstasy Through Tantra* (St. Paul, MN: Llewellyn Worldwide, 3rd. rev. ed., 1988), pp. 47–68 and associated color plates. Dr. Mumford discusses the classical postures, as well as oral and anal sex and khechari mudra.

CHAPTER 49. DOGGY STYLE
AND SOME NEW TRICKS

44. Michaels and Johnson, *The Essence of Tantric Sexuality*, pp. 123–25. The work of Dr. Stuart Meloy was reported on *Good Morning America*. "Doctor Discovers the 'Orgasmatron': Physician Working with Pain Relief Stumbles upon Delightful Side Effect." *Good Morning America*, ABC-TV, November 9, 2004. Meloy found that he could induce orgasm in an overwhelming majority of his subjects through electrical stimulation of the sacral nerve.

PART 9: EXPANDING ORGASMIC RESPONSE

45. Singh, trans., *The Yoga of Delight*, pp. 66–67. The Singh translation also includes the commentary.

46. The *Yoga Sutras* translation is from Mumford, *Ecstasy Through Tantra*, p. 32.

47. Dr. Jonn Mumford, *Sexual Tantra* (audio cassette) (St. Paul, MN: Llewellyn Publications, 1989).

48. Janniko R. Georgiadas and Gert Holstege, "Human Brain Activation during Sexual Stimulation of the Penis," *The Journal of Comparative Neurology* 493: 33–38 (2005). http://keur.eldoc.ub.rug.nl/FILES/wetenschappers/1/17556/human_2005.pdf. Accessed September 5, 2011.

49. Janniko R. Georgiadas et al., "Regional Cereberal Bloodflow Changes Associated with Clitorally Induced Orgasm in Healthy Women," *European Journal of Neuroscience* 24: 3305–16 (2006). Studies conducted at Rutgers University suggest that the left pre-frontal cortex shows increased activity during masturbatory and mentally induced orgasms. The reasons for this disparity are unclear, although the presence or absence of a partner seems like a plausible explanation. See Kayt Sukel, "Sex on the Brain: Orgasms Unlock Altered

Consciousness," *New Scientist* 2812: 6–7 (May 2011). http://www
.newscientist.com/article/mg21028124.600-sex-on-the-brain
-orgasms-unlock-altered-consciousness.html?full=true. Accessed
September 5, 2011. Sukel observes that "[d]espite orgasm being a
near-universal human experience, we still don't know that much
about it." We should learn a great deal more over the next few years.
Nan Wise, a PhD candidate at Rutgers University and a member of
the team that is on the cutting edge of this research commented: "The
exploration of these discrepancies will be the focus of my dissertation work. The biggest difference between the studies is the method-
ology used: PET (Georgiadas et al.) versus fMRI (Komisaruk et al.).
FMRI is by far a superior method when it comes to both spatial and
temporal resolution of brain activity. Another important point is that
Georgiadas et al. (2006) did not find significant activations of the
hypothalamus, striatum, or brainstem, areas which were shown to be
activated by Komisaruk et al. (2002, 2010) during orgasm, and would
be expected to play an integral role in orgasm and other rewarding
behaviors based on previous studies. I will use fMRI and have three
different conditions of orgasm for my dissertation study: self-stimulation (masturbation), partner stimulation (partner), and imagery
stimulation (without touch) to compare and contrast with special
attention to the frontal regions." Nan Jacobson Wise, email message
to authors, September 6, 2011.

CHAPTER 50. SIMPLY GIVE AND RECEIVE

50. Shaoni Bhattacharya, "Frequent Ejaculation May Protect Against
Cancer," *New Scientist* (April 6, 2004). http://www.newscientist.com
/article/dn4861-frequent-ejaculation-may-protect-against-cancer
.html. Accessed September 5, 2011. The study itself was published in
Journal of the American Medical Association 291:1578 (2004).

51. Barbara Carrellas, *Urban Tantra: Sacred Sex for the Twenty-First Century* (Berkeley, CA: Celestial Arts, 2007), pp. 165–200.

52. Joseph Kramer Productions, *Fire on the Mountain: An Intimate Guide
to Male Genital Massage* DVD (2006). Erospirit Productions, *Fire in
the Valley: An Intimate Guide to Female Genital Massage* DVD (2004).

53. Mark A. Michaels and Patricia Johnson, *Tantra for Erotic Empow-
erment: The Key to Enriching Your Sexual Life* (Woodbury, MN:
Llewellyn Worldwide, 2008), pp. 151–62. Michaels and Johnson, *The
Essence of Tantric Sexuality*, pp. 145–61.

54. The Alexander Institute, *Tantric Sexual Massage for Lovers* DVD (2008).

CHAPTER 52. ANAL SEX
FOR ENERGY ACTIVATION

55. Gopi Krishna, *Kundalini: The Evolutionary Energy in Man* (Boulder, CO: Shambhala, 1971). *Kundalini* is one of the seminal works on the purported dangers (which are also mentioned in some of the classical texts) of the Kundalini experience. Krishna's writing had a significant impact on Western thinking about the subject.

56. Tristan Taormino, *The Ultimate Guide to Anal Sex for Women* (Berkeley, CA: Cleis Press, 2nd ed., 2006). Tristan Taormino, *The Anal Sex Position Guide: The Best Positions for Easy, Exciting, Mind-Blowing Pleasure* (Beverly, MA: Quiver, 2009). Jack Morin, PhD, *Anal Pleasure and Health: A Guide for Men, Women and Couples* (San Francisco: Down There Press, 4th rev. ed., 2010).

CHAPTER 53. BREAK YOUR PATTERNS
TO DISCOVER NEW SENSATIONS

57. Nina Hartley and I. S. Levine, *Nina Hartley's Guide to Total Sex* (New York: Penguin, 2006), pp. 132–33. In the book, Hartley describes this form of sexual response by saying that she and some other women " . . . come once, hard, but it's not easy to get there . . . " She has used the exact phrase "hard come" in lectures we've attended.

Glossary

Achilles tendon: The fibrous tissue that connects the calf muscle to the heel.

Action organ: An organ that is associated with a specific chakra and through which that chakra expresses itself physically.

Aghora: Aghora means "without fear." The term refers to a Tantric sect that engages in extreme practices. Aghoris embrace that which most of society would find intolerable.

Alchemy/Alchemical: The transformation of matter or the process of combining two or more elements and creating a new substance.

Amrita: Literally, that which is against death: the nectar of immortality. In classical Tantric sex rituals, commingled sexual fluids that are consumed by the practitioners. Some Neo-Tantric teachers refer to female ejaculate as "amrita."

Amygdala: A group of almond-shaped nuclei located within the temporal lobes of the brain. The amygdala is involved in the processing of memory and emotional reactions.

Analingus: Using the mouth and, especially, the tongue to stimulate the anus.

Ananda: Commonly translated as bliss, but it can also mean happiness, joy, or sensual pleasure.

Ananda Nidra: Ananda (happiness, joy, bliss, sensual pleasure) Nidra (sleep). The authors developed this practice, which is inspired by Yoga Nidra, a traditional Tantric meditation.

Antinomianism: The rejection of socially established morality or religious laws.

Anuswara: Little heaven. The bindu or dot that sometimes appears above Sanskrit letters. It indicates prolonging and nasalizing the *m* or *n* sound. It is what gives simple mantras like Om their power to alter consciousness.

Aphrodisiac: Something that excites or produces sexual arousal.

Ardhapadamasana: The Half Lotus Posture: in this modified version of the Lotus Posture, only one foot is placed atop the thigh when the legs are crossed.

Areola: The area of rose-colored to dark pigmented skin surrounding the nipples.

Ashwini mudra: Literally, the "gesture of the horse." Ashwini mudra is the intentional pulsing of the anus. This practice is very important in many Tantric routines since it is a powerful way to raise energy within the body. It is also reputed to have a wide variety of health benefits.

AUM: Alternative transliteration of the syllable Om. It highlights the three sounds that compose the mantra.

BDSM: An acronym for a variety of sexual practices that include bondage, discipline, dominance, submission, sadism, and masochism.

Blasphemous: Disrespectful or disparaging of religious beliefs, irreverent, sacrilegious.

Bön: The indigenous religion of Tibet. It predates the arrival of Buddhist teachings in Tibet, but its current form has both influenced and been influenced by Buddhism.

Bondage: The use of restraints, real or imagined, for power exchange during erotic play.

Brahma: The creator god in the Hindu trinity.

Brahman: God, the supreme Godhead or universal soul. Despite the fact that Hinduism is described as a polytheistic religion, there are certain monotheistic aspects underlying the concept of Brahman. Interestingly enough, the literal meaning of the word means "growth" or "expansion."

Buddha nature: The definition varies somewhat in different branches of Buddhism, but it can be understood as suggesting that the potential for Buddhahood is intrinsic in all beings and that it can be awakened through practice.

Chakra: Disk or wheel. Chakras are energetic centers in the body that can be used as a kind of inner roadmap in Tantric practice. Dr. Jonn

Mumford defines a chakra as "a whirling vortex of energy, the meeting point between the body and the mind."

Cis-gendered: A person whose gender as defined at birth, anatomy, and self-identification all match. Compare with *transgendered.*

Coccygeal plexus: A cluster of nerves residing at the base of the spine.

Coccyx: The tailbone. The coccyx is comprised of the three to five vertebrae below the sacrum, at the very base of the spine.

Contact pedophiles: Adults who engage in sexual activity with children, as opposed to those whose activities are limited to fantasizing about it or viewing child pornography.

Cosmology: A way of explaining the universe and its processes. The word can be used in both scientific and religious contexts.

Cunnilingus: A form of oral sex in which the clitoris and labia are stimulated with the mouth and tongue.

Cupid's bow: The shape of the upper lip, a reference to the Roman god of love, an implicit recognition of the erotic appeal of that body part.

Digital stimulation: The use of the fingers to produce sexual arousal.

Dildo: A sex toy used for penetration; dildos are most often designed to evoke the penis.

Dualism: The division of the world into binaries: mind and matter, sacred and profane, subject and object.

Ecstasy: Bliss, an intense emotional state in which the individual is transported beyond the bounds of everyday consciousness.

Edging: The practice of remaining at the edge of orgasm for prolonged periods. Not to be confused with *edgeplay,* a term used by the kink community to refer to boundary-pushing activity.

Energy body: Also called the aura. The energetic field that surrounds the physical body; some believe it can be seen by the psychically gifted.

Energy orgasm: An orgasmic experience that can be felt throughout or in specific parts of the body, with or without genital involvement. It can be induced by breath, movement, sound, visualization, or any combination thereof.

Enlightenment: In Eastern religions, the experience of being free from the ignorance that causes suffering. Also, being released from the cycle of death and reincarnation. From the Tantric perspective, enlightenment is a process rather than a state.

Erectile tissue: A category of tissue found in the genitalia, nipples, and nose. Erectile tissue becomes engorged with blood during sexual arousal.

Erogenous zones: Parts of the body that are particularly responsive to sexual touch.

Ether: Akasha in Sanskrit, also translated as space. Akasha is the fifth element in Tantra and Yoga.

Exhibitionism: Deriving sexual pleasure from showing off to or being watched by others.

Fellatio: Oral sex performed on a penis (or sex toy).

Female ejaculation: A form of orgasmic response in which fluid, probably produced by the Skene's glands (which some anatomists now call the female prostate), is expelled through the urethra.

Fetish: A sexual fixation on a body part or an object, not necessarily something that is commonly considered erotic. Human beings have the ability to fetishize virtually anything.

Fleshlight: A flashlight-shaped tube that evokes female genitalia and is designed for use in masturbation.

Fluid-bonded: People who have agreed to share sexual fluids and are not using safer-sex protocols.

Foreplay: Sexual stimulation that usually precedes intercourse and is intended to build arousal. The term reflects the prevailing cultural assumption that anything short of genital intercourse is a mere precursor to the main event.

Frenulum: Most commonly, the highly sensitive part of the penis, where the foreskin connects with the glans, just below the opening of the urethra. The area remains sensitive in those who are circumcised. Frenulum generally refers to a small piece of tissue that connects body parts or holds one in place. Thus, the frenulum of the tongue is the tissue at the base of the tongue that attaches it to the floor of the mouth. Other body parts, including the labia minora, the clitoris, and the upper and lower lips (of the mouth) also have frenula.

Friction sex: A fast-paced style of lovemaking that usually has achieving orgasm rapidly as the goal.

Frottage: Rubbing the genitalia on an object or body part for the purpose of sexual arousal.

Full-body orgasm: A sexual response that may include but is not limited to the genital area. See also *Energy orgasm.*

G-spot: Not a spot at all, but an area of erectile tissue including the para-urethral glands, which surround the urethra and become engorged with fluid during sexual arousal. It feels like a ridge of rougher textured tissue, and it is located three to four inches inside, on the anterior (front) wall of the vagina.

Gender identity: The way a person self-defines—as male, female, neither, both, or some other category. This may or may not be congruent with biological sex or genitalia.

Glans: The head of the penis or clitoris.

GLBTQ: Gay, Lesbian, Bisexual, Transgender, Queer. An acronym that is widely used to describe people who do not identify with the conventional model of heterosexuality.

Heteronormative: The cultural tendency to define heterosexual behavior as normal, thereby marginalizing all other forms of sexual expression.

Hippocampus: A brain structure located in the medial temporal lobe. The hippocampus is part of the limbic system and is the part of the brain that governs spatial memory and navigation. Damage to the hippocampus can interfere with the ability to form new memories.

Homophobic: Fearful of nonheterosexual people and acts.

Hypothalamus: An almond-sized area of the brain located just above the brain stem. The hypothalamus regulates the autonomic nervous system and the pituitary gland, linking the nervous and endocrine systems. It controls body temperature, thirst, hunger, and circadian rhythms.

Hysteria: From the Greek for *uterus.* Hysteria was believed to be a psychological disorder until 1980, and for most of that time it was considered to be specific to women. Symptoms were said to include conversion of psychological stress into physical symptoms, emotional volatility, and self-dramatizing behavior. In the nineteenth century, the term was applied to what now is commonly called sexual dysfunction.

Hysterical paroxysm: A nineteenth- and early-twentieth-century term for female orgasm. Inducing it was seen as a way to relieve the symptoms of "hysteria." Doctors would "treat" their patients using mechanical or manual pelvic massage.

Impact play: A category of BDSM that uses the sensations triggered by spanking, flogging, punching, and other forms of striking to build sexual arousal and/or induce an altered state of consciousness.

Jainism: An Indian religion founded between the sixth and ninth centuries BCE. There is no creator deity in Jainism, which is similar to Hinduism and Buddhism in its belief in reincarnation and karma. Jains are noted for their commitment to nonviolence and their expansive understanding of that term.

Kali: One (for some, the supreme) manifestation of the divine feminine in Hinduism.

Kali Asana: A sexual position in which the person being penetrated is on top, astride and facing the person on the bottom.

Kama Marmas: Literally, love or desire points. Marma therapy, which is used in both Ayurvedic and Tamil medicine, is akin to acupuncture or acupressure. Dr. Mumford introduced a system of building sexual arousal using these points, and we describe it in detail in our book *The Essence of Tantric Sexuality.*

Kashmir Shaivism: The form of Tantra that is generally considered to be the most sublime and complex. The most significant scriptures were written between the sixth and twelfth centuries; Abhinavagupta is the most celebrated author of Kashmir Shaivite texts. The tradition has all but disappeared, due in part to the violence in Kashmir since the partition of India and Pakistan in 1947. Swami Lakshmanjoo was among the last great gurus of the tradition, and some of his disciples have carried the teachings forward. Daniel Odier also teaches a form of Kashmir Shaivite Tantra.

Kechari mudra: A Tantric and Yogic practice in which the tongue is placed behind the uvula, inside the nasopharynx (the space where the mouth and nasal passages meet).

Kegel exercises: Exercises of the pubococcygeal muscles, named for gynecologist Arnold Kegel, who "invented" them in the 1950s. Exercising the PC muscles was well known among Tantric and Yogic practitioners long before Kegel made his "discovery."

Kinesthesia: The sense that pertains to awareness of the body's position and movements.

Kriya Yoga: Kriya means "action," and Kriya Yoga practices generally combine subtle head movements, breathing techniques, mantra, and visualization to lead the practitioner into a meditative state. Paramahansa Yogananda was Kriya Yoga's best-known exponent in the West, but there are a number of other lineages. For a more in-depth discussion of Kriya Yoga and the term *Kriya,* see chapter 3 of our book *The Essence of Tantric Sexuality.*

Kundalini: An energy that is said to reside at the base of the spine. Awakening the Kundalini is one aim of Tantric and Yogic practices. Kundalini literally means "coiled," and it also has the implication of a pot. One way to understand Kundalini is to think of it as sexual energy. Another approach would be to define it as the life force that resides within all human beings.

Limbic system: A group of brain structures, including the hippocampus, thalamus, hypothalamus, and the amygdala, that control basic emotions and drives.

Lingam: Literally, "mark" or "sign," implying the mark or sign of the male deity. Thus, it also means penis. As a symbol, the lingam is associated with Shiva.

Lube: Short for *lubricant.* We encourage readers to use lube in their sexual encounters. There are many different products on the market. Lube may be water based, silicone based, or oil based. It is important to be aware that some kinds of lube may increase the risk of infection if they contain glycerin or certain oils. Silicone should never be used with a silicone toy, and oil-based products are also incompatible with latex—including gloves, condoms, and dental dams.

Macrocosmic: Large scale. Pertaining to the universe.

Manifesting: The practice of working with thoughts with the intention of bringing about material change in the world.

Mantra: Mind tool, from *manas* (mind) and *trayati* (tool). Mantras are words or sounds that serve to focus the mind or direct energy. Mantras can also function as incantations. They range from single-syllable Bija or seed mantras to being quite complex and multisyllabic. Mantras can be repeated mentally, under the breath, or as chants. Each method has its own unique impact on the mind of the practitioner and the physical environment. In his younger days Dr. Mumford was renowned for his ability to induce trance and imperviousness to pain in others by chanting a mantra, a technique he calls "Mantra Anesthesia."

Masochism: Finding pleasure, especially sexual pleasure, in experiences that are commonly deemed to be painful or humiliating.

Masturbation: Sexual self-stimulation.

Method acting: A style of acting inspired by the Russian teacher Constantin Stanislavski. It was adapted and popularized in the United States by Lee Strasberg. Method actors rely on their own emotions and memories when creating characters. *Sense memory* is one of the basic method acting exercises.

Microcosmic: Compare with *macrocosmic*. Small scale. In Tantric sexual ritual, practitioners seek to enact macrocosmic concepts on the microcosmic level.

Monotheistic: Believing in a single God.

Mudra: A gesture, most often of the hand, that has symbolic significance and that can bring about physiological or psychic changes in the practitioner. Also, a kind of parched grain that is used in the traditional Tantric sex ritual.

Mulabandha: Literally, "root lock." In Tantra and Yoga, the practice of tightening and holding the anal sphincter.

Nadi: In occult Tantric and Yogic anatomy, one in a system of psychic channels or nerves.

Nasal mucosa: The mucus membranes inside the nose.

Negative space: The space around and between objects. Most commonly used in reference to art.

Neo-Tantra: A term first used by Sir John Woodroffe and others in his circle in the context of their early-twentieth-century efforts to revive and reclaim the Tantric tradition. It is more commonly attributed to Bhagwan Shree Rajneesh (Osho), who used it to describe his system, which incorporated ideas and methods from a variety of sources, including other spiritual traditions and human potential movement psychology. Neo-Tantra is now used more generally, and sometimes disparagingly, to refer to Western forms of Tantra, particularly those that emphasize sacred sexuality and little or nothing else.

Neural pathway: The connection between one part of the nervous system and another.

Numinous: Containing divine power or divine presence, imbued with spirit. More generally: capable of evoking fear, trembling, and fascination.

Olfactory cilia: Hair-like filaments of the olfactory nerve that hang down into the nasal cavity and carry odors to the nerve for processing in the brain. The only part of the nervous system that is directly exposed to the environment.

Olfactory system: The components of the brain and nervous system responsible for the sense of smell.

Om: A symbol that predates written language. Om is often described as being the primordial sound; it is also called the primordial or liberation mantra. Chanting it, even just for a few minutes, can produce changes in consciousness.

One-pointed concentration: Ekagrata in Sanskrit. The capacity to focus intently on a single thing, without distraction.

Orality: Pertaining to the oral stage of development.

Orbitofrontal cortex: A region of the frontal lobes of the brain. Much remains to be learned about the orbitofrontal cortex, which is involved in planning, decision-making, and sensitivity to reward and punishment.

Oxytocin: A neurotransmitting hormone that influences orgasm, bonding, anxiety, and maternal behaviors from childbirth to breastfeeding.

Parasympathetic nervous system: The part of the nervous system that governs rest, relaxation, salivation, the production of tears, digestion, and excretion. See also *Sympathetic nervous system.*

Pelvic floor: The muscles and connective tissue that lie at the bottom of the bowl created by the hips. The pelvic floor supports the bladder, intestines, and uterus.

Perineum: In common usage, the perineum is the area between the anus and the genitals, although some define it as running from the coccyx to the pubic bone, encompassing the anus and genitals.

Philtrum: The groove that runs from the base of the nose to the top of the upper lip. From the Latin for "love potion."

Pituitary gland: A gland that is housed in the sphenoid saddle or *sella turcica* at the base of the brain. It is connected to the hypothalamus. It produces a number of hormones and controls the functioning of the entire endocrine system.

Prana: Most commonly used to mean the breath. Prana is understood as the energy that surrounds us and pervades the universe at all times. Another way of understanding Kundalini energy (see *Kundalini*) is to recognize it as each individual's highly concentrated dose of inborn prana.

Pranayama: Control or regulation of the breath, usually applied to various Tantric and Yogic breathing techniques. Since *prana* also refers to energy, another way to think about controlling the breath is to understand it as directing energy.

Prefrontal cortex: The front of the brain, including the orbitofrontal cortex. It plays a central role in complex cognitive functions, the expression of personality, and social behavior.

Prostate gland: A gland located at the base of the penis. The prostate surrounds the neck of the bladder and the urethra. While it is a gland, it also contains muscle tissue, and is surrounded by nerves. It plays an important role in erection, arousal, and orgasmic response; not only does it produce prostatic fluid, which makes up 20–30 percent of semen, but its smooth muscles also pulse during orgasm and play a significant role in expelling the ejaculate.

Pubic bone: The pubic bone is not actually a single bone. Instead, it is the front of the pelvis, where the left and right bones meet. It lies just above the genitals, well below the crest of the hips.

Pubococcygeal muscles: The muscles that form a part of the pelvic floor, also known as the "Kegel muscles" or "PC muscles." Learning to work these muscles in various ways is a key part of many Tantric and Yogic practices. More generally, exercising them is very important for urogenital health, in both men and women.

Reiki: A form of energy healing and spiritual practice developed in Japan by Mikao Usui in the 1920s. Its Western form has become very popular in recent decades.

Reverse cowgirl: A sexual position in which the person being penetrated is on top of, astride, and facing the feet of the person on the bottom.

Root lock: See *Mulabandha.*

Sacrum: The sacrum is usually composed of five bones in the lower spine that start to fuse in adolescence and have usually become fully fused in young adulthood. These are the spinal bones that pass through the pelvis. The sacrum lies between the bones of the lumbar spine, above, and the coccyx, below.

Sadism: From the Marquis de Sade. Deriving pleasure, especially sexual pleasure, from inflicting physical or emotional pain on others.

Safer sex: Sexual practices intended to reduce the risk of spreading or catching sexually transmitted infections. Most commonly this involves the use of barriers—condoms, dental dams, and gloves—for activities in which exposure to sexual fluids would otherwise occur.

Sahajoli mudra: Literally, the "spontaneous gesture." In some traditions it is synonymous with vajroli mudra; in others, it refers to the female version thereof. In either case, it involves the pulsation of the muscles around the urethra.

Sanskrit: The ancient language of India. Many Tantric texts were written in Sanskrit, although some were written in regional languages.

Sanskrit is still the language of Hindu ritual, although it is no longer living as a conversational tongue.

"Secret language": Pulsing the pubococcygeal muscles back and forth during penetrative intercourse.

Sensory avenue: The sense that is associated with a particular chakra.

Shakti: Goddess, particularly the Goddess in the form of energy. It also refers to a goddess in her role as consort to a male deity and hence to a female participant in Tantric sex rituals.

Shanka Nadi: Literally, "conch channel." In occult, Tantric anatomy, a psychic nerve that is said to run from the philtrum to the clitoris. While the mechanism for this function appears to be unknown to Western science, our own experience and observations suggest that many people will feel a mild genital response when the philtrum is stimulated, and this is true regardless of gender.

Shava: Corpse. It is said that Shiva (Consciousness) is a corpse without Shakti (Energy).

Shiatsu: A Japanese bodywork technique that focuses on energetic flows, akin to acupressure.

Shiva: Male deity, one of three gods in the Hindu trinity, often described as the god of destruction and the lord of the yogis. Shiva is the most important male deity in modern Tantra.

Siddhas: Perfected ones. A term for Tantric practitioners. Most commonly used to refer to the South Indian, Tamil Siddha tradition.

Sikh: A follower of an Indian religion founded by Guru Nanak in fifteenth-century Punjab. Sikhism is monotheistic but shares many philosophical precepts with Hinduism and Buddhism. The gurus of the Sikh tradition appear to have been influenced by Sufism and Bhakti (devotional) Hinduism.

Sine qua non: A Latin phrase that means "without which not." In other words, an essential or the essential element.

Solar plexus: A network of nerves located in the abdomen. In Tantra, the location of the third chakra, the area between the base of the rib cage and the navel.

Sphenoid sinus: The sinus that lies at the top and back of the nasal passages, just below the sphenoid saddle, which houses the pituitary gland. Chanting a mantra properly sends vibrations through the sphenoid sinus and into the pituitary.

Sukhasana: The Easy Pose. Sitting cross-legged.

Swami: Literally, "one's own master," a reference to being released from conventional social obligations. Traditionally, swamis were celibate and either resided in monasteries or would wander and teach and depend on alms for their sustenance. Some modern reformers have modified the requirements and have initiated women and married people as swamis.

Sympathetic nervous system: The part of the nervous system that is responsible for the "fight or flight" response. It complements the parasympathetic nervous system, and the two must be functioning harmoniously for sexual arousal and orgasm to take place. See also *Parasympathetic nervous system.*

Tantrika: A Tantric practitioner. In some contemporary circles, the term has become associated with practitioners of "Tantric massage."

Taoism: A Chinese spiritual tradition that shares some common elements with Tantra, including the recognition of sexuality's sacred dimension. In the broadest terms, Taoist sexual practices focus more on health and longevity than on attaining mystical states. In the Taoist system, there is frequently an emphasis on non-ejaculatory sex or on limiting ejaculatory frequency for men, based on the belief that the semen contains vital energy that must not be depleted.

Thankas: Tibetan Buddhist religious paintings.

Thinking off: Inducing orgasm through mental activity alone.

Tibetan Buddhism: The form of Buddhism that is practiced in Tibet, although the term is often applied to Buddhism indigenous to other Himalayan countries and Mongolia. The Tibetan Buddhist tradition is, for the most part, Tantric.

Trataka: To gaze without blinking. A technique for developing one-pointed concentration. It can be practiced on a candle flame, a yantra, a statue of a deity, or upon your beloved.

Twilight language: A way of writing characteristic of Tantric texts. It is intended to obscure the meaning of those texts, thereby preventing the uninitiated from grasping them.

Ulnar nerve: The nerve that runs along the ulna (one of the bones of the forearm). The largest unprotected nerve in the body, it produces a sensation commonly called "hitting one's funny bone" when directly bumped.

Umami: Japanese term for the fifth taste, sometimes called savory. It is often described as the taste that makes people want to eat more of something. Glutamic acid is the chemical that is responsible both for the flavor and the effect.

Upanishads: A series of over two hundred sacred texts that have played a significant role in shaping the Hindu tradition. Some were composed more than 2,500 years ago.

Urethra: The tube that stretches from the bladder to the genitals, and through which one urinates.

Vagus nerve: One of the nerves responsible for orgasmic response. It is also referred to as the *pneumogastric nerve.* It regulates heart rate, peristalsis, and sweating, and because it does not reach the lower body through the spinal column, some people whose spinal cords have been severed can still experience orgasm when it is stimulated.

Vajroli mudra: The contraction of the muscles around the urethra near the base of the penis. See also *Sahajoli mudra.*

Vibrator: A mechanical device for massage and/or sexual stimulation. Its original purpose was to make it easier for nineteenth-century doctors to induce "hysterical paroxysms" in their patients.

Vira: Hero, the type of personality suited for Tantric sexual practice. A person of heroic temperament is energetic and active, with a courageous nature, the key element being action.

Vishnu: The sustainer or preserver god in the Hindu trinity. Vishnu is believed to have incarnated in many forms, most notably as Krishna and Rama.

Voyeurism: Deriving sexual pleasure from watching people in various stages of undress and/or in sexual activity.

Vulva: The external uro-genital area of the female.

Yab Yum: (Tibetan) Father—Mother. It refers to the classical Tantric lovemaking posture, in which the person on the bottom sits in the lotus position (or a modified form thereof) with a partner astride.

Yantra: Tool for conception; a geometric figure with spiritual and symbolic significance. Yantras can be quite simple—a triangle, a square, a crescent—or quite complex.

Yoga: Yoking or union; an Indian spiritual tradition closely related to Tantra. While most Westerners think of Yoga as a form of exercise characterized by various *asanas* (postures), there are many ways to practice Yoga, and some of them do not involve physical postures at all. It can be useful to think of Yoga as a state of mental stillness, accompanied by a feeling of union or merger with all that is.

Yoga Nidra: Yogic sleep. A Tantric technique first introduced to the West by Paramahansa Satyananda Saraswati in the 1960s. Yoga Nidra involves the rotation of consciousness through the body and various visualizations. It produces a deep state of relaxation, in which the mind often remains quite alert.

Yoni: The female genitalia, including the womb.

Yoni Asana: A sexual position similar to Yab Yum, except that the person on the bottom is seated on the edge of a bed or chair, feet firmly on the floor.

Bibliography

Advanced Tantric Sex Secrets (DVD). Sherman Oaks, CA: The Alexander Institute, 2008.

Auguste, Annie. "The History of Fellatio." *Salon*, May 22, 2000. http://www.salon.com/sex/feature/2000/05/22/oral_history/print.html.

Barrs, Patchen. *The Erotic Engine: How Pornography Has Powered Mass Communication, from Gutenberg to Google.* Toronto: Anchor Canada, 2010.

Bhattacharya, Shaoni. "Frequent Ejaculation May Protect Against Cancer." *New Scientist*, April 6, 2004. http://www.newscientist.com/article/dn4861-frequent-ejaculation-may-protect-against-cancer.html.

Birnbaum, Molly. *Season to Taste: How I Lost My Sense of Smell and Found My Way.* New York: HarperCollins, 2011.

Brody, Stuart, and Rui Miguel Costa. "Vaginal Orgasm Is More Prevalent in Women with a Prominent Tubercle of the Upper Lip," *The Journal of Sexual Medicine*, June 15, 2001. Abstract: http://onlinelibrary.wiley.com/doi/10.1111/j.1743-6109.2011.02331.x/abstract.

Carnes, Patrick. *Don't Call It Love: Recovery from Sexual Addiction.* New York: Bantam, 1992.

———. "The Ten Types #1—Fantasy Sex," http://www.iitap.com/documents/SDI-R%20The%20Ten%20Types%20-%20Long%20Version.pdf.

Carrellas, Barbara. *Urban Tantra: Sacred Sex for the Twenty-First Century.* Berkeley, CA: Celestial Arts, 2007.

Comfort, Alex, trans. *The Koka Shastra and Other Medieval Indian Writings on Love*. New York: Stein and Day, 1965.

Conlee, Turhan, and John D. E. Gabrieli. "Imaging Gender Differences in Sexual Arousal." *Nature Neuroscience* 7:4 325–326, 2004. http://homepage.psy.utexas.edu/Homepage/Group/MestonLAB /Publications/brain.pdf.

Daedone, Nicole. *Slow Sex: The Art and Craft of Female Orgasm*. New York: Grand Central Publishing, 2011.

Dodson, Betty. *Liberating Masturbation: A Meditation on Self-Love*. New York: Body Sex Designs, 1974.

———. *Self-Love and Orgasm*. New York: privately printed, 1983.

———. *Sex for One: The Joy of Self-Loving*. New York: Harmony Books, 1987.

Dupuche, John R. *Abhinavagupta: The Kula Ritual as Elaborated in Chapter 29 of the Tantraloka*. Delhi, India: Motilal Banarsidass, 2003.

Eagleman, David. "10 Unsolved Mysteries of the Brain: What We Know—and Don't Know—About How We Think." *Discover Magazine*, August 2007. http://discovermagazine.com/2007/aug/unsolved-brain -mysteries/article_view?b_start:int=0&-C.

Fire in the Valley: An Intimate Guide to Female Genital Massage (DVD). Oakland CA: Erospirit Productions, 2004.

Fire on the Mountain: An Intimate Guide to Male Genital Massage (DVD). Oakland, CA: Joseph Kramer Productions, 2006.

Friday, Nancy. *My Secret Garden: Women's Sexual Fantasies*. New York: Trident, 1973.

Galinsky, Adena N., and Freya L. Sonenstein. "The Association of Developmental Assets and Sexual Enjoyment Among Emerging Adults." *Journal of Adolescent Health*. 48:6, 610–15, June 2011.

Georgiadas, Janniko R., and Gert Holstege. "Human Brain Activation during Sexual Stimulation of the Penis." *The Journal of Comparative Neurology* 493:33–38, 2005. Georgiadas, Janniko R., R. Kortekaas, R, R. A. Nieuwenburg, J. Pruim, A. A. Reinders, G. Holstege. "Regional Cereberal Bloodflow Changes Associated with Clitorally Induced Orgasm in Healthy Women." *European Journal of Neuroscience* 24: 3305–16, 2006.

Goudrian, Teaun, ed. *Ritual and Speculation in Early Tantrism: Studies in Honor of André Padoux*. Albany: State University of New York Press, 1992.

Hart, Karen. "Face Reader; Rose Rosetree, 58, Sterling." *The Washington Post*. June 18, 2006, M3.

Hartley, Nina, with I. S. Levine. *Nina Hartley's Guide to Total Sex*. New York: Penguin, 2006.

Herring, Bill. "What Is Sexual Sobriety?" July 10, 2009. http://billherring .info/atlanta_counseling/definition-of-sexual-sobriety.

Horgan, John. "The God Experiments." *Discover Magazine*, December 2006. http://discovermagazine.com/2006/dec/god-experiments /article_view?b_start:int=1&-C.

"How to Tell If You Have a High Sex Drive." http://answers.yahoo.com /question/index?qid=20080403161048AAIpgM8.

Howard, Hillary. "Vibrators Carry the Conversation." *New York Times*, April 21, 2011. E1.

Kelliher, Kevin. http://www.sci.uidaho.edu/biosci/labs/kelliher/Research .htm.

Krishna, Gopi. *Kundalini: The Evolutionary Energy in Man*. Boulder, CO: Shambhala, 1971.

Ladas, Alice Kahn, Beverly Whipple, John D. Perry. *The G Spot and Other Discoveries About Human Sexuality*. New York: Dell, 1982.

Lerner, Jonah. "The Subjectivity of Wine." *Scienceblogs*, November 2, 2007. http://scienceblogs.com/cortex/2007/11/the_subjectivity_of _wine.php.

Lu, Henry C. *Traditional Chinese Medicine: How to Maintain Your Health and Treat Illness*. Laguna Beach, CA: Basic Health Publications, 2005.

Lundström, Johan M., Julie A. Boyle, Robert J. Zatorre, and Marilyn Jones-Gotman. "The Neuronal Substrates of Human Olfactory Based Kin Recognition." *Human Brain Mapping* 30:8, 2571–80, August 2009.

Maines, Rachel P. *The Technology of Orgasm: "Hysteria," the Vibrator, and Women's Sexual Satisfaction*. Baltimore, MD: Johns Hopkins University Press, 2001.

Media Matters for America. "Conservative Media Continue Tired Obsession with Obama's Supposed 'Bowing.'" April 13, 2010. http:// mediamatters.org/research/201004130016.

Michaels, Mark A., and Patricia Johnson. *The Essence of Tantric Sexuality*. Woodbury, MN: Llewellyn Worldwide, 2006.

———. *Secrets of Sacred Sex: The Essence of Tantric Sexuality*. Delhi, India: Motilal Banarsidass, 2011.

———. *Tantra for Erotic Empowerment*. Woodbury, MN: Llewellyn Worldwide, 2008.

Monier Williams, Sir Monier. *A Sanskrit-English Dictionary: Etymologically and Philologically Arranged with Special Reference to Cognate Indo-European Languages*. Oxford: Oxford University Press, 1899, repr. 1979.

Morin, Jack. *Anal Pleasure and Health: A Guide for Men, Women and Couples*. San Francisco: Down There Press, 4th rev. ed., 2010.

Mumford, Jonn (Swami Anandakapila Saraswati). *A Chakra and Kundalini Workbook: Psycho-Spiritual Techniques for Health, Rejuvenation, Psychic Powers and Spiritual Realization*. St. Paul, MN: Llewellyn Worldwide, 3rd rev. ed., 1999.

———. *Ecstasy Through Tantra*. St. Paul, MN: Llewellyn Worldwide, 3rd. rev. ed., 1988.

———. *Sexual Tantra* (audio cassette). St. Paul, MN: Llewellyn Worldwide, 1989.

Northrup, Christiane. *Women's Bodies, Women's Wisdom (Revised Edition): Creating Physical and Emotional Health and Healing*. New York: Random House, 2010.

"Oprah Talks Masturbation." *The Huffington Post*, January 17, 2008. http://www.huffingtonpost.com/2008/01/17/oprah-talks-masturbation_n_82070.html.

"Question: Is the Usage of Toys Allowed During Sexual Intercourse?" *Catholic Writings*, http://catholicwriter.wordpress.com/2006/09/13/question-is-the-usage-of-sex-toys-allowed-during-sexual-intercourse/.

Restak, Richard. *The Secret Life of the Brain*. Washington, DC: Joseph Henry Press, 2001.

Richardson, Diane. *Slow Sex: The Path to Fulfilling and Sustainable Sexuality*. Rochester, VT: Destiny Books, 2011.

Robbins, Dale A. "About Sex and Marriage." http://www.victorious.org/sex.htm.

Sackheim, H. A., R. C. Gur, and M. C. Saucy. "Emotions Are Expressed More Intensely on the Left Side of the Face." *Science*, 27 October 1978, 202 (4366): 434–36.

Saraswati, Swami Satysangananda. *Sri Vijnana Bhairava Tantra: The Ascent*. Munger, India: Yoga Publications Trust, 2003.

Saraswati, Swami Yogakanti. *Sanskrit Glossary of Yogic Terms*. Munger, India: Yoga Publications Trust, 2007.

Sheldon, Kerry, and Dennis Howitt. "Sexual Fantasies: All in the Mind." *The Times* (London), online edition, February 7, 2007. http://women .timesonline.co.uk/tol/life_and_style/women/relationships /article1341377.ece?token=null&offset=0&page=1.

Shore, Joan Z. "Politically Correct Sex (for Women)." *The Huffington Post,* January 22, 2008. http://www.huffingtonpost.com/joan-z-shore /politically-correct-sex-f_b_82689.html.

Silburn, Liliane, Jacques Gontier, trans. *Kundalini: Energy of the Depths.* Albany: State University of New York Press, 1988.

Singh, Jaideva, trans. *The Yoga of Delight, Wonder, and Astonishment: A Translation of the Vijnana-bhairava.* Albany: State University of New York Press, 1991.

Sukel, Kayt. "Sex on the Brain: Orgasms Unlock Altered Consciousness." *New Scientist* 2812:6–7 May 2011. Online at http://www.newscientist .com/article/mg21028124.600-sex-on-the-brain-orgasms-unlock -altered-consciousness.html?full=true.

Tantric Sexual Massage for Lovers (DVD). Sherman Oaks, CA: The Alexander Institute, 2008.

Taormino, Tristan. *The Anal Sex Position Guide: The Best Positions for Easy, Exciting, Mind-Blowing Pleasure.* Beverly, MA: Quiver, 2009.

———. *The Ultimate Guide to Anal Sex for Women.* Berkeley, CA: Cleis Press, 2nd ed. 2006.

Torraco, Stephen F. "Is It a Sin for a Married Couple to Have Oral Sex with Each Other?" EWTN, Global Catholic Network. Online at http:// www.ewtn.com/vexperts/showmessage.asp?number=507442&Pg= Forum5&Pgnu=1&recnu.

Urban, Hugh B. *Tantra: Sex, Secrecy, and Power in the Study of Religion.* Berkeley: University of California Press, 2003.

Webb, Nadia. "The Neurobiology of Bliss—Sacred and Profane: Sex in the Brain and What It Reveals about the Neuroscience of Deep Pleasure." *Scientific American,* July 12, 2011. Online at http://www .scientificamerican.com/article.cfm?id=the-neurobiology-of-bliss -sacred-and-profane.

"What Does a Kiss on the Neck Mean." FreeDating411.com. http://www .freedating411.com/kissing/What-Does-A-Kiss-On-The-Neck-Mean .html.

White, David Gordon. *Kiss of the Yogini: "Tantric Sex" in Its South Asian Contexts.* Chicago: University of Chicago Press, 2006.

Index

GET MORE AT LLEWELLYN.COM

Visit us online to browse hundreds of our books and decks, plus sign up to receive our e-newsletters and exclusive online offers.

- Free tarot readings • Spell-a-Day • Moon phases
- Recipes, spells, and tips • Blogs • Encyclopedia
- Author interviews, articles, and upcoming events

GET SOCIAL WITH LLEWELLYN

Find us on   @LlewellynBooks

www.Facebook.com/LlewellynBooks

GET BOOKS AT LLEWELLYN

LLEWELLYN ORDERING INFORMATION

 Order online: Visit our website at www.llewellyn.com to select your books and place an order on our secure server.

 Order by phone:
- Call toll free within the U.S. at 1-877-NEW-WRLD (1-877-639-9753)
- Call toll free within Canada at 1-866-NEW-WRLD (1-866-639-9753)
- We accept VISA, MasterCard, American Express and Discover

 Order by mail:
Send the full price of your order (MN residents add 6.875% sales tax) in U.S. funds, plus postage and handling to: Llewellyn Worldwide, 2143 Wooddale Drive Woodbury, MN 55125-2989

POSTAGE AND HANDLING

STANDARD (U.S. & Canada):
(Please allow 12 business days)
$30.00 and under, add $4.00.
$30.01 and over, FREE SHIPPING.

INTERNATIONAL ORDERS:
$16.00 for one book, plus $3.00 for each additional book.

Visit us online for more shipping options. Prices subject to change.

FREE CATALOG!

To order, call
1-877-
NEW-WRLD
ext. 8236
or visit our
website

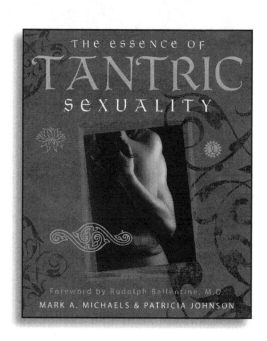

THE ESSENCE OF

TANTRIC

SEXUALITY

Foreword by Rudolph Ballentine, M.D.

MARK A. MICHAELS & PATRICIA JOHNSON

THE ESSENCE OF TANTRIC SEXUALITY

Mark A. Michaels and Patricia Johnson

In 1976, Dr. Jonn Mumford gave a series of groundbreaking lectures on sexual Tantra at the annual Gnosticon Festival. Over thirty years later, his teachings still resonate. Based on Dr. Mumford's pioneering work, *The Essence of Tantric Sexuality* introduces Tantric theory and practice—revealing powerful techniques that, until now, have been kept secret.

From autoerotic mysticism to sex magic, this book reveals how internal energies can be used to reach altered states of consciousness and transcendence. Much more than an erotic sex manual, this book also carefully explains the Tantric philosophy and the principles of this Indian tradition, effectively demystifying Tantra and making it accessible to beginners. Erogenic zones, perfume magic, secret Tantric symbols, Tantric massage, the Tantric mass, and Tantric terminology are all explored in this comprehensive guide to sexual Tantra.

978-0-7387-0900-0, 240 pp., 7½ x 9⅛   **$19.95**